B Street

THE NOTORIOUS PLAYGROUND OF COULEE DAM

LAWNEY L. REYES

UNIVERSITY OF WASHINGTON PRESS

SEATTLE AND LONDON

B Street

THE NOTORIOUS PLAYGROUND OF COULEE DAM

B Street *is published with the assistance of a grant from the Naomi B. Pascal Editor's Endowment, supported through the generosity of Janet and John Creighton, Patti Knowles, Mary McLellan Williams, and other donors.*

© 2008 by the University of Washington Press
Printed in the United States of America
Designed by Pamela Canell
12 11 10 09 08 5 4 3 2 1

University of Washington Press
P.O. Box 50096, Seattle, WA 98145 U.S.A.
www.washington.edu/uwpress

Library of Congress Cataloging-in-Publication Data can be found at the back of the book.

The paper used in this publication is acid-free and 90 percent recycled from at least 50 percent post-consumer waste. It meets the minimum requirements of American National Standard for Information Sciences—Permanence of Paper for Printed Library Materials, ANSI Z39.48–1984.♾♲

FOR JULIAN, MARY, AND HARRY

All things are connected. Whatever befalls the earth befalls the children of the earth.

—ATTRIBUTED TO CHIEF SEALTH, SUQUAMISH *&* DUWAMISH

CONTENTS

PREFACE

As early as 1918, a few men in eastern Washington State realized that the arid land of the great Columbia basin needed water. They reasoned that the land, rich in itself, would never be worth much until it could be irrigated. Elbert F. Blaine of Grandview came up with the idea of irrigating the Grand Coulee valley. He suggested that water could come via a canal from the Pend Oreille River and that the water would be drawn to the Grand Coulee by gravity, simply because of the change in elevation.

In 1919, William M. Clapp, an attorney from Ephrata, met with a few others in town and discussed matters of local importance. The talk soon centered on how the Grand Coulee was formed when glaciers dammed the Columbia River, diverting water into the canyon. Clapp suggested that if nature had once dammed the river, nothing could stop men from doing the same thing with concrete. The water could be pumped five hundred feet up from the Columbia River to the level of the Grand Coulee and stored in Banks Lake, a man-made reservoir. From there, canals could distribute the water to the lands of the Great Columbia Plain. The men thought about Clapp's idea and agreed that he had offered a most interesting concept. This plan became known as the "pumping plan" and was supported by residents of Wenatchee and of smaller towns such as Ephrata, Moses Lake, Pasco, and Quincy.

Now there were two different ideas for irrigating the arid land, Elbert Blaine's gravity plan and William Clapp's pumping plan. The two plans were hotly debated during the 1920s. The Spokane Chamber of Commerce and the Washington Water Power Company supported the gravity plan. They did not want competition from anyone, especially the United States government, in supplying hydroelectric power to consumers in the region. The people in Wenatchee and the smaller towns favored the pumping plan. They were interested in helping those who were not rich. They reasoned that revenues from hydroelectric power would eventually pay for the costs of irrigating and thus help the farmers who were having a difficult time. Supporters of the pumping plan promoted the idea that reclamation could be achieved by constructing a dam. They pointed out that the sale of hydroelectric power to a growing number of people moving into the area would pay for the costs. They proposed locating the dam at the north end of the Grand Coulee on the Columbia River.

To many in eastern Washington, this seemed like a pipe dream; when the Great Depression hit in 1929, the plan was placed on the back burner for many. One third of the nation's labor force was without work. Most lived from day to day, concentrating on merely surviving from one day to the next. No kind of work or way of obtaining a few dollars was looked down upon, and nearly everyone accepted ways of surviving that, before the hard times, they had deemed beneath them or unacceptable. It became obvious that Washington State was in need of large-scale employment.

In 1931, the Bureau of Reclamation became interested in building a dam on the Columbia River, but President Herbert Hoover's administration was having problems with the Depression and was

Washington State map locating Grand Coulee near the Columbia River. Courtesy Lawney Reyes and Kroll Map Company.

trying to balance the budget. A few favored the construction of a dam, but that idea was set aside for a later date, after the economy had improved. Help from the federal government appeared unlikely.

Rufus Woods, editor of the *Wenatchee Daily World* newspaper, could not dismiss the idea of a dam at the Grand Coulee, and an attorney, James O'Sullivan, who had moved to the area from Michigan, joined Woods in his ongoing pursuit. The idea fascinated him, and he devoted his life to making the dream a reality. Eventually, Woods and O'Sullivan, with the backing of others, were able to get support from many in the state of Washington and, finally, the needed endorsement from Olympia, the state capital.

In time, their efforts paid off at the federal level when President Franklin D. Roosevelt signed the bill into law. Roosevelt was aware at the time that large numbers of men could be put to work building a dam, easing the problem of high unemployment in the Northwest. He also knew of the potential of the Grand Coulee. He knew the land was rich and ready for planting. All it needed was a great amount of water, a design for implementation, and a lot of money, and it would be able to support many farmers and their families.

The construction of a low-rise dam, with designs to accommodate a future high-rise dam that would provide for irrigation at the Grand Coulee, became a reality in 1933. Roosevelt persuaded Congress to provide blanket public works funding that his administration could direct to the construction of the dam. This legal maneuver allowed 150 workingmen and engineers to begin work in 1933 and also enabled Roosevelt to authorize construction of a high-rise dam.

Afterward, many came to the Grand Coulee area to seek their fortunes. Small-time entrepreneurs leased lots and constructed, as best they could, small buildings to house their places of business. As more men were hired to work on the initial construction of the dam, card sharks, prostitutes, pimps, taxi dancers, and hustlers appeared. They all became energetic regulars on what came to be known as B Street. The street was located on a bench, or ridge, to the west of and two blocks above Midway Avenue, the main thoroughfare of the little town of Grand Coulee. This unusual street was rapidly being constructed to accommodate the hundreds of young men who were arriving daily seeking work.

During the thirties, from 1933 to 1941, The Street became home to many from different walks of life. Hundreds, then thousands of white men came from different parts of the country to find work. As the numbers of laborers increased, entrepreneurs set up a variety of small businesses along the street. It became a place where a family of Indians, down on their luck, created a business and was able to make a modest living. It was a place where a small number of young Indian men found a new way of life after gaining employ-

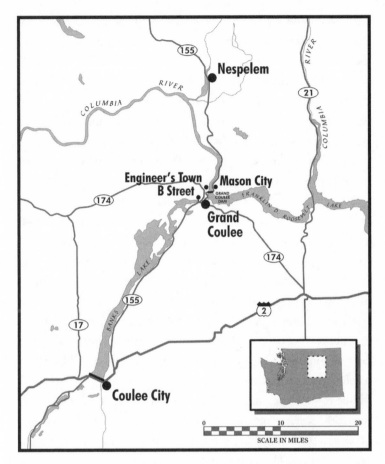

Grand Coulee Dam and surrounding communities between Nespelem and Coulee City near the Columbia River. Courtesy Lawney Reyes and Kroll Map Company.

ment in the gravel pits at the dam site. Still later, after experiencing much discrimination, some four dozen Negroes were hired to work at demeaning, and also the lowest-paying, jobs. It became home to a man from China who found work at what he did best and, eventually, owned his own business. It became a haven for numerous women who were able to support themselves and escape the poverty of the times.

From the beginning, The Street was the place to play and let off steam for thousands of white workingmen who had faced the hard times of the Depression. It was a raucous playground that denied Negroes, and some Indians whose skin was too dark, access to the frivolity, prostitutes, and good times that were the main attractions of that provocative place.

The stories of B Street are the accounts of real people from diverse racial, cultural, and social backgrounds. They were the ones most affected by the Great Depression. The stories tell of hard times, struggles, courage, and goals and reveal the humor, toughness, and recklessness of those adventurous people who came to Grand Coulee to make a living during the difficult times of the thirties.

Because I didn't want the story of B Street, and the other stories that are related to it, to be lost to history, it seemed important to capture some of that past and put it into writing. I once heard that when seniors pass on, a piece of history goes with them. In this book, I hope to preserve and share a unique and boisterous way of life that took center stage during the 1930s in the Grand Coulee area of eastern Washington State. It is a way of life I still remember from my early years. The stories that follow are about real people and real events that took place on B Street, one of the wildest and most outrageous streets in the United States at that time.

ACKNOWLEDGMENTS

I want to acknowledge the stories told to me by my dad, Julian, after I had grown up. They reinforced my memories of those early years. Harry Wong also shared stories about living in Grand Coulee. Much later, Dewey Hall told me of his adventures and good times when he worked and played there. The personal diary of my mother, Mary, imparted a wealth of information about B Street and the Inchelium area. These were given credence by talks with Edo Quill, my mother's best friend.

Most of the accounts of Luana, Pickles, and myself come from my memories of those days, which are still a part of me. My older cousin Eneas Boyd and his friend Antoine Paul substantiated these and related stories with their recollections.

Dennis King, a resident of Grand Coulee, helped in the early stages of this book. He showed me several photographs of the construction of the dam along with others of B Street in the early days. He took time to explain them to me. A number of these photographs appear in the book. Dennis shared stories he had heard about the dam. He told me about the last salmon runs, past the dam, that occurred in 1938 and introduced me to men who had worked on the dam and run businesses during that time. Some of these men still live in the Grand Coulee area.

Chuck Hall and his wife, Linda, provided other material. Chuck was the general foreman for Vinnell Construction Company, a subcontractor at the dam site. He was in charge of cleanup and concrete. Chuck shared important information about the construction of the dam, and Linda recalled life around Grand Coulee Center during the construction days. She informed me that she steered clear of B Street because of the things that went on there but shared her overall insight on Grand Coulee and the nightly activities on B Street.

Bill Miller, a resident of Electric City, voiced other memories. He was the foreman of mechanics for the Bureau of Reclamation. Bill was in charge of ordering supplies for all internal combustion engines, such as trucks, cranes, and forklifts. He shared information on the construction of the dam and talked about a number of his experiences on B Street.

Jean Nicholson, a Grand Coulee historian, provided a wealth of information on Grand Coulee Center and B Street. She had lived in the area and could remember what happened year by year. Jean has written articles about the Grand Coulee area. She was like a walking history book. Her husband, Jack, was a newspaper boy during those times and made deliveries to the Woo Dip restaurant. He offered other information about the ladies of the night and how he grew to value their kind treatment of him. Both Jean and Jack shared their recollections and encouraged me to write this book.

Trudi Tonasket, a teacher at the high school in Inchelium and a member of the Lakes (Sin-Aikst) Tribe, introduced me to the Ceremony of Tears. She also found important photographs of Inchelium that she shared with me, one showing the Columbia River rising. Two of these are in the book. This helped bring my stories full circle and provide a proper ending.

Important old photographs were given new life through the diligent and professional ability of Bob Morrisson. His editing and restoration of the photos are an essential part of this book. I wish to extend my gratitude to Bob for his valuable input.

Rod Hartman, a resident of Grand Coulee, provided information about the Roosevelt Theater in Grand Coulee when his father managed it. He explained that the theater provided entertainment to the residents of both Grand Coulee and B Street.

Therese Kennedy Johns deserves most of the credit for the completion of this book. She devoted days, weeks, and months that turned into years to the refinement of the manuscript. She aided me immensely with her advice, creativity, research, and fact finding. Therese was the initial editor of the work. This book is as much hers as it is mine.

I also want to thank University of Washington Press editors Marilyn Trueblood and Laura Iwasaki and designer Pamela Canell for their thoughtful help in producing this book.

Finally, I must express my appreciation to Naomi Pascal, former editor-in-chief of the University of Washington Press. Her meaningful and continued guidance directed me in finding my way.

INTRODUCTION: THE GRAND COULEE

A determined wind swept up the coulee, moving dust and debris as it went. Small whirlwinds formed here and there, defined by the dust they carried. They zigzagged up the sloping hill from one spot to another to the bench above. They lingered briefly, whipping sagebrush and wild grass about them. Then they would continue on and die as quickly as they were born.

Now and then, jackrabbits appeared and then loped off in great strides with eyes ever alert and long ears straining to hear threatening sounds from coyotes looking for prey. As they ran, they sometimes scared up coveys of sage hens that swiftly flew out of harm's way. Rattlesnakes, looking for prey, slithered down to the ravine en route to the protective canyon below that bordered the swift-flowing Columbia River.

Ground squirrels were positioned as sentinels in front of their places of residence, alert for any apparent danger. Birds also seemed to prefer the tree-covered canyon. They flew quickly above the bench and the sloping hill, stopping only to catch insects that thrived on the sagebrush. Over the centuries, these activities occurred with little change within this community of beings.

Sagebrush and wild grass dominated the hill, and rocks peeked out of the soil here and there. Minute caravans of insects busily scurried off to somewhere more to their liking. The sloping hill and bench had always been a thoroughfare for living things searching for a friendlier and more accommodating place to spend their time.

The bench above was nondescript, as it had been for centuries. It was hardly noticeable, lying at the base of hills to the northwest just above the place where a great dam would one day be constructed. A ravine below bordered the sloping hill that led to the bench. It was inviting and took travelers down to Rattlesnake Canyon and the river below. Short, stout, disfigured pine trees stood alone or in small groups surrounding the canyon. They looked as if they had always been there. One could imagine that these rugged-looking trees had struggled for life and won the right to be in that challenging landscape.

Over the centuries, hunters and gatherers of different tribes quietly moved with the seasons, and other beings, like deer and coyotes, carved subtle trails along the ravine as they traveled east or west. During the late 1700s, white fur trappers traveled these same trails on their way to the northeastern part of what is now Washington State and, farther north, British Columbia. The wildlife that lived there was a community within itself and had adjusted to the area. This diverse community was made up of beings that had adapted to their place in life and treated it with care and respect.

When white people came through the area for the first time, one could sense the beginning of change. These driven and determined beings would view their surroundings unaware of what had happened before them. They would not believe that a community of others could live for centuries without disturbing the natural balance and beauty of this unusual landscape.

During the 1870s and 1880s, more white settlers came in their wagons, driving small herds of livestock along the ravine as they traveled down to the river below. The nearly invisible trails became ravaged and torn as iron wheels and the foreign hoofs of unfamiliar beasts cut through and trampled the rich grass. Once across the river, the settlers sought land for building homes and established meager settlements, creating change that would eventually disrupt the beautiful landscape.

A few settlers remained in the southern end of the Grand Coulee near what is now Coulee City. They tried working the rich soil but soon realized that they needed water. They hoped that reclamation would compensate for "nature's failure." Some of those early people sensed that the Columbia River might one day provide water, and many farmers would reap the benefits of the excellent farmland.

Later, other white men came to settle the land. Minor skirmishes with Indians in the area slowed settlement. After the government subdued the Indians, more settlers came to the Columbia Plateau. A number brought cattle and sheep. They also introduced wheat in the Soap Lake and Moses Lake areas, but in time, the moisture gave out and the organic content of the soil was reduced. The soil became susceptible to erosion. In an effort to conserve what moisture there was, the settlers planted only half of the acreage annually. The fallow half absorbed water from rain and snow and was planted the following year. In the early part of the twentieth century, people planted fruit orchards, but, once again, the moisture gave out, and most of the settlers left.

Development followed slowly because the harsh land presented great difficulties to those who tried to settle it. The weather was hot in the summer and very cold in the winter. The winds were strong and created aggravating dust storms during the spring and early summer. Inland, away from the river, there was little water for irrigation.

Before the appearance of white men, a small spring seeped from a hillside where Midway Avenue now borders the small town of Grand Coulee, which was founded in the ravine where animals, Indians, and other travelers had created a trail. The cool water from the hillside spring quenched the thirst of all who journeyed through the area. During the late 1920s, when white men began to settle the area, they installed a fifty-five-gallon steel tank to capture the water. Later, Ida Bartels, an early resident and promoter of the Grand Coulee area, installed a small pump that enabled easier access to the water.

Ida had moved from Rock Island, Washington, and bought land that she would later sell to others who came to live in the Grand Coulee area. She was instrumental in helping to establish a small community and later a town. Ida devoted a great deal of time and effort to improving living conditions in the area. She made important contacts with state government officials who later supported her effort to establish Grand Coulee as a viable place that would someday become a self-supporting town. As the small community slowly grew, schools, a hospital, and the city government came into being because of her efforts.

No one in those early days expected much of the Grand Coulee area. Those who came to live there were happy with the solitude they found in the struggling town. Most were modest farmers. A few were ranchers who raised small herds of cattle. They grew to accept the endless acres of sagebrush and the wildlife it fostered. Survival was hard, but the residents adjusted to the extreme weather that came with the change of seasons. There were no signs to indicate that this was a land of promise.

B Street

THE NOTORIOUS PLAYGROUND OF COULEE DAM

1

MOCCASIN TELEGRAPH

Early in the morning, during late spring of 1934, Antoine Paul saddled two of his horses, a bay and a black, which he always kept in a small corral near his cabin. He was a tall, lanky man of twenty-one years. He had straight dark brown hair, and his complexion was medium bronze. Antoine had a narrow aquiline nose that reminded one of the beak of an eagle. His deep-set dark eyes and high cheekbones revealed his Sin-Aikst ancestry.

Antoine led the horses from the corral. His legs were slightly bowed from years of riding horses. He mounted the bay easily and rode effortlessly, as if born to ride, his frame swaying in rhythm to the bay's gait.

Antoine led the black past the town of Inchelium that morning on his way to meet Eneas Boyd, his friend. Inchelium, a community of about 250, bordered the Swah net ka (Columbia River) on the Colville Indian Reservation, about seventy miles upriver from the Grand Coulee. Antoine and Eneas had spent their entire lives there.

Eneas would accompany Antoine hunting in the hills above the little town. Antoine rode his bay slowly, methodically drawing on

Inchelium viewed from across the Columbia River, 1938.
Courtesy The Spokesman-Review.

his handmade smoke as he led the black along the outskirts of town
and then north along the Swah net ka.

The rough pine houses in Inchelium showed a variety of knots
in the siding, decorating the buildings in a pleasing natural way.
The unpainted siding had aged and turned varying degrees of dark
brown and gray over the years. Rusted nail heads dotted the lumber. In some places, the shanks of rusted nails were visible, pulled
by the breathing and buckling of uncured lumber over the decades.
The small houses all had tarpaper roofs that had aged to a soft gray.
They had the appearance of having been built by the same person.
There was a similarity about them that seemed to suggest they might
be in some way related.

Tepees here and there indicated that some of the residents were still doggedly adhering to traditions. Outhouses placed close to the houses suggested that they were companions in need. Antoine smiled as he remembered that during Halloween the outhouses were the first to go. Young people did not go trick-or-treating because no one had anything to give. But boys would go around at night, after most people were asleep, and tip over the outhouses. He remembered doing that himself when he was young. Antoine also remembered how angry the adults became when they discovered the young boys' misdeeds the following morning.

A few of the houses had wooden fences around them, not always in the best of repair. There were no manicured lawns, no exotic deciduous trees, except for the chokecherries, willows, and occasional serviceberries that lined the Swah net ka. A few lilac bushes contributed beauty and fragrance to the town. An occasional pine tree shaded houses that were close by. A huge forest of pine, fir, and tamarack surrounded the little town, dotted here and there by groves of aspen. Wild grass, cheatgrass, and an assortment of weeds covered the areas surrounding many of the houses. Hard-packed trails had been formed by years of use where constructed walks might be expected.

Smoke rose from disfigured, rusting metal stovepipes of various shapes, indicating that breakfasts were being prepared for the houses' occupants. This seemed like a typical day in Inchelium, which Antoine had witnessed so many times before. Things did not seem to change much. Everyone knew one another, and most were related in some way. The future always seemed predictable. Antoine mused as his mind dwelled on this.

As he rode past, he thought that Inchelium looked better in the winter when the town was covered with a blanket of snow. At that time of year, especially at night, the town was peaceful and quiet, lying under millions of stars. The snow reflected the brilliance from above. Warm dim lights, from kerosene lamps glowing through windows, gave evidence of life in the little town. Smoke rising quietly from stovepipes seemed to warm the town and link everything to the sky above. The occasional barking of dogs echoed the howls of coyotes in the hills. The powerful rumbling of the Swah net ka, as it surged its way south, was the only continuous sound.

When he was a boy, he often wondered what compelled the Sin-Aikst and the Swhy al puh to choose Inchelium as their permanent home. Now that he was older, he knew that the tribes had been forced to live here. All of their land to the north had been taken from them.

The two tribes had nearly been wiped out by smallpox in the 1800s. The Sin-Aikst had once been a tribe of two thousand but, because of the white man's disease, were reduced to a little more than three hundred people. The Swhy al puh, their neighbors, had not done much better. Since that time, the two tribes were linked and worked closely together. Their language and customs were basically the same. They became known as the People.

Both tribes were part of the Colville Confederated Tribes along with ten others: the Nespelem, Okanogan, San Poil, Palouse, Nez Perce, Wenatchee, Chelan, Methow, Moses, and Entiat. All of these tribes lost their homelands to white people throughout the state of Washington and were corralled on what is now the Colville Indian Reservation.

Losing so many people to smallpox weakened the Sin-Aikst and the Swhy al puh. There were not enough warriors left to defend the tribes. When the Blackrobes came to spread the gospel, the two tribes were basically down and out. Their traditional belief in the spirit powers was no longer strong. The chief of the Sin-Aikst, Kin ka Nawha, was convinced that he did not have the power to help his people during those years. He endorsed Christianity and worked to have his tribe accept the teachings of Christ. When this happened, the Sin-Aikst lost all resistance to change and became dependent on the white man and, eventually, his way of life.

When Antoine was still a young boy, he wondered why his tribe and the Swhy al puh became sick with the white man's disease. He wondered why his people could not resist the illness and death. Antoine was not sure who was to blame for the disaster. He wondered if the spirits had been angry with his people and punished them for their misdeeds. He thought about the powers of the white man. Were they greater than the powers of his people? These were big questions for young Antoine, and he could not find answers that satisfied him.

Since that time, people in Inchelium gradually became accustomed to their plight. A pattern of living came to be, and over the decades, everyone adjusted to it. Every year was a direct reflection of the year before. Change became a forgotten element. As time went on, the traditions were gradually dismissed. Soon the language was forgotten. Only a few elders were fluent. When this happened, the Sin-Aikst culture was on its way to becoming history. By the time the U.S. government changed the tribe's name to Lakes in the mid-1880s, the culture and the traditions were little more than memories.

Antoine remembered when the elders of his tribe talked about the white man coming into their country. At first, the newcomers were small in number, but as time went on, the increase was alarming. He often wondered where they all had come from. Their numbers could be gauged by the destruction that followed. The loss of trees upriver of Inchelium, near Kettle Falls, in the northern half of the reservation, was the most evident. Soon, only stumps remained where great forests had once stood. Witnessing the destruction was devastating for the People who were so much a part of the forests.

He often wondered why the Sin-Aikst had not grown in number. Two thousand people did not seem to be a lot, now that he thought about it. Antoine did not realize that his people had adjusted to nature long ago, like other beings of the forest. Their numbers had always been in harmony with the environment. They grew in balance with the other beings and in keeping with what the environment could sustain. As he thought about it, he agreed that was a good thing. It was something to appreciate. Some believed the powers of the Great Spirit controlled the numbers of the People. The Sin-Aikst were comfortable with this thought. They believed in the wisdom of this great force, this great power.

When the miners came, their excavations left huge amounts of soil and rocks piled to one side as they disemboweled hillsides and mountains. These were the actions of people with no respect for Mother Earth, who were feverishly searching for minerals of worth. Tribal members who hunted were surprised to see so many holes dug into the sides of the mountains, marking great wounds on their mother earth.

Antoine rode three miles upriver to where the Boyd family lived. Eneas was chopping wood in front of his house, preparing fuel for the stove inside. He had removed his shirt, and his lean hard body glistened as he worked. Eneas was the same age as Antoine and close to six feet tall. His features were Indian, but his fair complexion and his wavy hair indicated that he carried white blood. Over the last five years, he had developed a muscular physique as a fighter. He fought on cards at smokers that were held in Kettle Falls and as far away as Spokane. Five of his younger brothers were his sparring partners. They were nearly as good at boxing as Eneas.

Eneas could see Antoine riding toward him in the distance. He raised an open hand, a form of greeting that his people had used for centuries. This gesture showed there would be no animosity and no concealed weapons.

Eneas poured a cup of strong black coffee into a battered tin cup and handed it to Antoine as he dismounted. Antoine took it and seated himself on a block of wood in front of the small house. He could see Eneas's mother, Agnes, and sister, Clara, through the window of the house. They waved, and Antoine smiled and nodded.

Antoine and Eneas sat quietly watching the river. They drank in silence as the Swah net ka surged powerfully past them.

Antoine studied the river. He noticed that there were fewer and fewer salmon, and he wondered how long this would continue. He did not know then that a smelter upriver, at Trail, British Columbia, was dumping lead, zinc, and other poisons into the river. He did not know that the smelter had been doing that for nearly thirty years, poisoning everything in the Swah net ka, including many salmon. He was not aware that the river was undergoing major changes seventy miles downriver, at Grand Coulee, and would one day be dead. This was all happening as Antoine and Eneas sat and drank their coffee, studying the river.

Antoine set his empty cup aside, stood up, and stretched his lean body. He suggested that they start riding.

Eneas placed his foot in the stirrup and hefted himself into the saddle of the black. He levered his .22 and checked the breech before securing the buckskin thong, tied to the rifle, on his right shoulder. Eneas thumped the black on its flank with his right heel as the horse bolted forward.

As they rode at the edge of the town, Inchelium gradually awakened. Adults, children, and their dogs emerged from their houses to welcome the first rays of sunlight. A rooster crowed at the far end of town; another answered it close by. The pecking of a woodpecker echoed in the forest surrounding the town. The sounds seemed to accent the gait of the horses' hoofs as they rode.

A young boy was pumping water into a bucket at the town pump in the middle of Main Street. Eneas remembered with a smile how he and his friends plugged the spout with mud when he was a boy. How surprised and angry the adults were when they pumped muddy water into their buckets. Over the years, the pump had rusted to a pleasing bronze color. The handle was worn smooth by years of use. The pump, which had been handled by generations of townspeople, had developed a warm, beautiful glow.

Indian women, mostly elders, emerged from their houses. Many of them wore their traditional dress, their heads tightly wrapped in bandanas. Braids rested softly on their breasts or sometimes hung down their backs. Their skirts, cinched with a leather or beaded buckskin belt, covered their legs. High-top moccasins, beaded at the top of the instep, finished off their attire. They all seemed to walk at a common tempo. A few had homemade smokes clamped firmly between thin lips, their expressions purposeful. Sometimes, the women carried buckskin purses, woven intricately with colored beads. At other times, the bags were of woven roots and displayed subtle geometric designs. Children, with their dogs close behind, followed the women as they walked from one house to another.

A number of the women moved quietly along a hillside aglow with patches of sunflowers, tiger lilies, and wildflowers. They were heading north to the hills that overlooked the Swah net ka. Antoine remembered seeing them en route to the fields where bitterroot and camas thrived. The women would harvest them and bring them home to dry, usually from mid-April to the end of May, depending on the weather and the amount of rain that had fallen.

Bitterroot and different varieties of camas were important staples for the People. Blue camas, called "black camas," was the most prized, but white camas was avoided because it was poisonous. These traditional roots went well with other foods. The women would gather and save them for the cold months, when food was hard to get. Antoine had seen the women in his family go to the fields in the spring and gather the roots all of his life. Sometimes, he had accompanied them and watched as they carefully removed the top layer of soil with sharp pointed sticks. Once exposed, the bulbs and roots were gently removed and placed in hand-woven baskets. The layer of soil was replaced. This had been a common practice of the women for centuries.

Teams of horses pulling wagons stirred pockets of dust as they slowly traveled Main Street. Some wagons went to pick up hay for the livestock that were corralled in town. Other wagons carried men and boys to work in the fields and forests outside of town, where some would cultivate alfalfa and others would cut dead logs into firewood.

A few old cars and pickups stirred up greater clouds of dust. The unpleasant noises of the untuned motors were foreign to the town of Inchelium. Older cars that had stopped running were simply abandoned where they had broken down. More than a dozen were parked here and there in their final resting places. Some were so rusted and dusty that it was difficult to tell how long they had been there. At times, children playing hide-and-seek used the cars to shield themselves from sight. When rain fell, the old cars provided dry shelters where the young could carry on long and searching discussions about life.

Now and then a car, covered with dust and marked with dents and blotches of rust, went to the landing and took the small ferry to Gifford. At other times, cars from across the river drove off the ferry and traveled on Main Street carrying white people on their way to Twin Lakes, about twelve miles west in the mountains. The white people's cars were highly polished and gleamed in the sunlight. There was always a great contrast between the cars owned by whites and those that belonged to Indians. The white people usually ignored this disparity and concentrated only on reaching the mountains. They loved to fish for the large rainbow trout at their favorite retreat, Twin Lakes. Some vacationed there for a few weeks, in resorts designed for white people only.

Cashmere St. Paul sat straight-backed on the raised wooden boardwalk in front of the General Store, wearing his fringed buckskin vest along with his colorfully beaded moccasins. He was puffing contentedly on a handmade smoke, his ever-present white flour sack at his side. The sack was Cashmere's holster and concealed his semiautomatic Colt .45. Everyone acknowledged that he was a fine hunter and would-be warrior and always gave him a wide berth.

Cashmere was considered the premier elder in the town; he was admired and respected by everyone. No one knew his exact age for sure, but most believed him to be well past his mid-eighties. He seemed to be the first one to awaken in Inchelium and could always be found on the boardwalk in front of the General Store. He was there as the first rays of sunlight appeared over the mountains. Cashmere was considered the guardian of Main Street.

A few other elders sat with him and talked in their traditional language, Sin-Aikst, as the warmth of the sun blanketed the town. Their conversation was barely audible as they spoke in low tones. They seldom looked at one another as they conversed. Sometimes, there would be soft laughter as they shared jokes or stories of the past.

Antoine and Eneas greeted the elders with a nod. Cashmere's

keen eyes, shaded by the brim of his dark brown high-domed reservation hat, followed them as they rode past.

Eneas and Antoine had hunted together many times. They first hunted on horseback when they were eight years old, just like other boys their age in Inchelium. The two did not have saddles in those days and had become expert riders. They guided their mounts with pressure from their knees and seldom used the reins. A shift of weight or a nudge from the knee was enough to direct the horse. It was as if the horse and the rider were one.

They would tie buckskin thongs to their .22s. Eneas rode with an old Remington that held a clip, and Antoine hunted with an ancient .22 Stevens single shot. One shot was usually enough for Antoine. He had owned the rifle since he was a young boy and was deadly accurate with it. The two carried the rifles strapped to their shoulders. The shores along the Swah net ka, north and south of Inchelium, were their hunting grounds. Sometimes, they hunted in the lower hills above town for small game. If they hunted deer, they went up into the lower mountains. As time went on, they became expert marksmen and skilled hunters who usually made the kill with the first shot. They could easily hit their targets from their horses, even while they were moving.

As they rode, Antoine thought about white people. He searched for answers and pondered why white people acted as they did. Antoine knew this was a big country; he wondered why white men had wanted all of it. He thought there was enough for everyone. Antoine could not understand why the leaders of the white people, the U.S. government, always backed those who took their land. He could not understand why the white people were not restrained or punished when it was obvious they were wrong.

Antoine had a difficult time understanding why white people had to change a land that he considered perfect. He saw no reason to change something that needed no change. When Antoine grew older, he understood that white people and their elected leaders were simply driven by greed. He learned that they did not consider mother earth a paradise. The whites thought of it as something to use to make a profit. That is the main reason his people and the Swhy al puh now lived in Inchelium. They had been pushed off land to the north and in the Colville Valley. That was the land white men considered valuable, and they wanted all of it.

Eneas saw two red-tailed hawks circling high in the sky. They drifted easily with the wind as they searched for prey. To Eneas, it looked as if they were marking time. When Eneas saw red-tailed hawks flying, it always gave him a feeling of impermanence, that life was fleeting. He could not explain why he felt this way, but he always sensed that something was on the verge of change. It was an uncomfortable feeling that he kept to himself as he rode with Antoine.

As they approached the higher benches above Inchelium, Antoine focused on things closer to the earth. In the distance, up on a hill, he saw some white men working. They were driving wooden stakes into the ground with blunt hammers.

Antoine reined in. He studied the white men intently as his horse reached for the wild grass around them. Eneas rode up and watched quietly and questioned why the men were up there. Antoine beckoned to Eneas to follow him and spurred his horse to a gallop. As they came upon the three white men, he noticed that one was marking numbers on a stake with a dark crayon.

One of the white men removed his hat and wiped his brow. A brief conversation left Antoine and Eneas surprised and greatly concerned. The white men had been hired by the Bureau of Reclamation to mark the future level of the river. The marks showed how high the river was expected to rise when the Grand Coulee Dam was completed.

Eneas looked at the stakes and then at the town below. He looked at the Swah net ka flowing in the distance and then at the white men, confused. Slowly, he realized that the town of Inchelium would be covered by the Swah net ka.

Antoine was overwhelmed when he realized what he was hearing. The news stunned him. He had heard something, more than a year ago, about a dam being built but had paid little heed. Someone from Nespelem had mentioned that the dam was to be constructed at the head of the Grand Coulee. Most of the people in Inchelium didn't take the news seriously. No one realized that the river would rise to cover the entire town.

The two rode back to town in silence. They had lost the urge to hunt that day. Both were deep in thought, trying to fathom the idea of a dam being built downriver and the water rising to cover their town.

They reined in at the front of the General Store and left their horses untethered. Cashmere studied them as they walked up the steps. He could detect the anxiety on their faces. He was surprised they had returned so early from hunting. Quietly, Cashmere followed them into the store, his curiosity awakened.

Inside the store, some people were buying merchandise. Others were sitting around the unlit pot-bellied heater, the favored meeting place in Inchelium. Some were smoking handmade smokes. As Antoine related what he had learned, most in the store thought he was inventing a story merely to unsettle them. He assured them that this was no laughing matter.

Antoine walked over to the counter and withdrew a small sack of tobacco from his shirt pocket. He rolled a smoke quickly and easily with one hand. He lit it and inhaled, then let the smoke out slowly as he thought. He finally suggested a town meeting to discuss the problems the People would soon face. He thought it wise that those who lived in the small communities near Inchelium and along the Swah net ka also attend. Everyone in the store nodded in agreement.

The moccasin telegraph worked effectively that day. By late afternoon, nearly everyone in the town of Inchelium knew about the meeting that was to be held on Friday night. A number of volunteers went in old cars and pickups and on horseback to share the news with families who lived upriver and in the hills and lower mountains. A few traveled as far as Round Lake and Twin Lakes to advise the families that lived there; others visited the small communities of Kewa and Covada, a short distance south of Inchelium. They told of the scheduled meeting, a meeting that would prove to be the most important town hall meeting ever held in the little town of Inchelium.

2

THE TOWN HALL

On Friday night, shortly after 6:00 P.M., people began arriving at the General Store. They were quiet and serious as they entered the building. There was no lighthearted horseplay or laughter as there usually was at large gatherings. Everyone seemed to sense that a very important meeting was to take place.

The town of Inchelium rarely received any news of significance, but when it did, the People would assemble at the General Store. The store was commonly referred to as the town hall, and many of the meetings that at first seemed important usually turned out to be of little interest. The People didn't mind, since, over the years, they had become accustomed to such results. But they welcomed any assembly because it gave everyone an opportunity to have a get-together, and they could exchange news, no matter how minor, with others. Talking and sharing news had always been the most important entertainment for people in Inchelium. Everyone looked forward to it.

The meeting scheduled to discuss the rising of the Swah net ka and the flooding of the little town of Inchelium promised to be of great importance. Wagons arrived at the General Store from various directions, hauling members of the tribe. Some individuals came on horseback. Families that had always formed the backbone of the community were there: the Toulous, the Seymours, the DeSautels, the Marchands, and the McClungs. Other important members of the tribe arrived later, including the Finleys, the Jerreds, the Michels, and the Stones. The Gendrons, the Lemerys, and the Noyes and Bass families came loaded into a few cars and pickups. Charlie and Eliza Hall with their son, Dewey, and Jerome and Florence Quill with their offspring, Moops, Mike, Jim, Gerlie, and Edo, were among the last to arrive.

Florence was a respected elder in Inchelium. She was in her early seventies, and her composure was always purposeful and straightforward. Her mission in life was to protect the interests of her people, the Sin-Aikst. Now that Chief James Bernard was ailing, she had become the principal spokesperson of the Inchelium community. She was articulate and fluent enough in the Swhy al puh and Sin-Aikst tongues that the elders could understand what she was saying.

Alec Covington had volunteered to chair the meeting. After everyone was seated, he asked Florence to take the floor. She immediately asked Antoine and Eneas to go over in detail what they had learned from the white men who were working on the upper benches above Inchelium. She wanted everyone in the General Store to hear firsthand how the young men had learned the news.

Florence studied Antoine and Eneas evenly as they spoke. After they were finished, she remained quiet, in deep thought. There was absolute silence as she sat there, eyes staring at the floor. Florence finally looked up and then rose to address the People with a determined look on her face.

She began her talk with a brief history of Inchelium. She felt it important to inform the young why they all lived in the little town. She reminded everyone that the government had forced the People into the area because it had taken all of their land to the north. The government, she informed her audience, was now about to take what was left of their land by covering it with water.

"The People, the Swhy al puh and the Sin-Aikst, had to tolerate the white man's greed," Florence explained. "As the years went by, our tribe began to lose everything. At one time, the land of the Sin-Aikst stretched from Kettle Falls to nearly two hundred miles north of Revelstoke, B.C. It was great country. The People were a tribe of several bands; they were always close to the Swah net ka and the Kettle River.

"At the beginning of the century, things turned for the worse. In about 1912, people from Russia came to the Castlegar area, a religious sect called Doukhobors. I hear there were over five thousand of them. These trespassers from another country began to take up Sin-Aikst land in what is called today the Brilliant area. One of our favored families, the Christian family, lived there. Their forebears had lived in Brilliant for centuries. It was a beautiful place to live, along the Kootenay River. The salmon and the game in the valleys and mountains were plentiful. Somehow, the Doukhobors came up with a piece of paper stating they now owned the land and wanted the Christians to move from the area. The Christian family was confused. They had never sold the land they lived on. They would never sell the land of their forebears."

Florence's eyes searched out the faces of the young listeners as she continued speaking. "White Grizzly Bear, his mother, Antoinette, and his brother, Baptiste, wrote many letters to the provincial government asking authorities to turn the land they were living on into an Indian reservation. They thought this would help them maintain ownership. The government, over time, ignored the letters and requests of the Christian family. The town of Castlegar made no attempt to help them.

"During August of 1913, the Christian family took their annual journey to Red Mountain near Rossland, B.C. It was the season for gathering huckleberries. While they were there, one of our very own, Mary Christian, was born. When they returned to their home in Brilliant, the Doukhobors had placed a barbed wire fence around their property. In the process, they plowed the land and demolished the family's headstones. From that time on, there was no way to discern where each of the family's ancestors was buried. Since their dwellings were fenced off, the Christian family land could be reached only by the waters of the Kootenay.

"Later, to conceal its treachery, the provincial government declared the Sin-Aikst an extinct people, with no land and no rights. After several members of the Christian family died, some went to live with and be a part of the Shuswap Tribe, northeast of Castlegar. The remainder, the families of White Grizzly Bear and his brother, Baptiste, moved south to the Kettle Falls area, to become a part of the Colville Tribe.

"At one time," she continued, "the land of the Swhy al puh included the million and a half acres north of this reservation. It extended all the way to the Canadian border. Their land also included the entire Colville Valley, with its great farmlands, where the town of Colville sits now. The People were great farmers. But white settlers wanted their land, and the U.S. government gave it to them after moving the Swhy al puh to the west side of the river, where hardly anything grew. Although they still fished Kettle Falls, they had really lost that, too. All the land around the falls was now claimed by white settlers."

In a soft voice, Florence continued her history lesson for the young members of the tribe. "Once the salmon runs were great, especially during June when the chinook came. The Salmon Chief would stand below the Falls and welcome the salmon. He would bless their arrival and thank them for the food they would provide for the People. Many tribes came at that time and pitched their tepees on both sides of the Swah net ka. The site was full of horses and wagons as the tribes came. It was a beautiful place when the Sin-Aikst canoes came from upriver. They were everywhere, above the Falls, going from one shore to the other."

Cashmere had lived through those times and knew what Florence was talking about. He responded with a nod of his head, as did other elders seated at the back of the store.

"Cashmere and the elders had known and ridden with James Bernard, White Grizzly Bear, and others of that time. They knew of the leadership of See Whel Ken, the good times and then the bad, under Kin Ka Nawha and Aropaquin, when they were nearly wiped out by the white man's disease. When the People lost the understanding of the spirit powers and accepted the foreign religion, Christianity, the strength of the tribe was essentially lost. The elders experienced it all, but a lot of the people now living know little of this, especially the young."

Florence paused briefly and accepted a small jar of water. She sipped the water slowly and thoughtfully and then continued. She reminded everyone that if the town of Inchelium was covered with water, Kettle Falls would also be covered. That would mean the end of all salmon runs. Florence predicted that the assembly of tribes at Kettle Falls would never happen again. She added, almost in a whisper, "If Kettle Falls and Inchelium are covered, the graves of our loved ones, along the river, will also be covered."

Florence took a deep breath and looked about the gathering of people. There was silence in the General Store. Outside, those who had not been able to get in strained to hear what was being said. Florence's voice held signs of anger as she spoke of the dam being built downriver. The east end of the Grand Coulee Dam would be attached to the Colville Reservation. Florence was angry that those who were responsible didn't have the decency to consult and listen to the People before approving this enormous structure.

From time to time, Florence talked in Sin-Aikst, so that the elders could understand what was being said. Others in the crowd who could speak the language did the same, and the elders would nod and say "hou" to let the young know that they understood. When Florence finished, she sat down. There was absolute quiet in the General Store.

Antoine leaned over and told Eneas that everything Florence had said was true. Florence was able to voice what the people were thinking. Eneas agreed. They were fortunate to have her here to speak for them.

Alec Covington got up and affirmed Florence's words. He thanked her and then opened the floor to questions, suggestions, or comments.

Several rose to ask questions or suggest strategies for preventing the flooding of Inchelium. When individuals spoke, there were no interruptions. The People respected the thoughts and opinions of others. This enabled everyone to understand what others thought and believed in. At the end of the meeting, Florence advised that the first order of business would be to contact the Colville Business Council in Nespelem, to see if they might find a way to persuade politicians in Olympia, and even Washington, D.C., to change course in the matter.

At the end of the meeting, Antoine sat outside the General Store with Eneas and Dewey. He rolled a smoke, lit it, and thought quietly. Finally, when he was done, he ground out the smoke and stood. Antoine seemed resigned. He felt that when dealing with white people, one never seemed to know where it would all end. The tribe had lost nearly everything. The Inchelium Indians were the poorest of the poor. They still had Kettle Falls, but it looked as if that would soon be taken from them. Over the last years, the salmon runs had become smaller and smaller. Once the Swah net ka rose and flooded the Falls and the town of Inchelium, everything would be lost.

In the days that followed, during that year in 1934, Florence learned that President Franklin D. Roosevelt had authorized the construction of a low-rise dam. She learned that the business council in Nespelem had been aware that a dam might be built as early as 1932. The council had resisted the idea at first but soon realized it was powerless. Once the decision had reached the federal level, it was fruitless to resist. The council and the People in Inchelium did not know at that time that their town would be covered by water when the Grand Coulee dam was completed and the river rose.

Florence wrote letters to representatives and lawmakers in Olympia, inquiring about how to prevent the flooding of Inchelium and Kettle Falls. She sent letters to the senators who represented the state in Washington, D.C. Florence had Moops drive her to Nespelem so she could talk to the Colville Confederated Tribes Council about the matter. As time was to prove, no one could help her. The president of the United States had approved federal funding to construct the dam, and cofferdams for diverting the flow of the river were already being built.

In the years that followed, the people in Inchelium struggled, barely surviving from day to day. They tried to sustain what remained of their culture and the semblance of their ways of living. Because of the dwindling salmon runs in the Swah net ka, many turned to the whitefish and perch that still remained. Other fish, like rainbow and eastern brook trout, caught in lakes and streams, began to replace the salmon. Most of the People's food now came from the game they hunted and whatever berries and roots they could harvest. Commodities provided by the government, such as beans, cornmeal, flour, and other staples, became necessities.

Many went up into the hills and searched for places where they could move their houses before the river rose. There was always a feeling of discontent and insecurity. All could foresee the end of a way of life. Others knew that a tribal culture, centuries old, was on the verge of disappearing.

3

FAMILY PLANNING

Julian Reyes and his wife, Mary, attended several town hall meetings in Inchelium during the summer and fall of 1934. They listened closely to what was said but still could not believe all that they heard. They discussed the matter at length with others. After all of the talk, there was still confusion. No one really knew what to do next.

The same question arose each time they returned home from the meetings. Where would they move when the town was covered with water? Mary was full of questions as she sat at the kitchen table.

Julian was deep in thought as he watched her. No one knew, at this point, what to do. He had no idea where they could move. He was not even sure if their house was strong enough to withstand a move, nor did he know how it could be moved.

Julian went into the kitchen and poured himself a cup of coffee. He returned, sat at the table, and drank slowly, absorbed in his thoughts. At the last meeting, Dewey Hall told everyone that he had heard the river would rise soon after the dam was finished. It might happen in 1941. If that were true, they would have about six years to prepare. Julian felt there was a more pressing issue: money. He had been looking for a job, any job, to get them through the winter. It was very hard to find work in Inchelium. It was hard to find work anywhere. After all, he explained to Mary, the country was in the midst of a serious depression.

Mary drew from her smoke and, with a degree of contempt, stated that there had been a serious depression for Indians in this country ever since the white man came. Julian walked to the door and looked out at the street. He thought deeply about the problems they faced. He found it hard to believe that this street would soon be underwater.

He remembered when he first met Mary. She was only a young girl of sixteen. They met when he happened to cross on the ferry between Gifford and Inchelium. He had never been on an Indian reservation before, and he was curious. Julian met Mary at the General Store that day, and there was an immediate attraction. In spite of their age difference, they seemed to have many things in common. Mary was impressed that Julian owned a car. It was an old, weather-beaten Model T Ford, with many dents, but Mary appreciated it because only a few people in Inchelium owned a car. Horses or horse-drawn wagons provided almost all the transportation in the area. After a few months of friendship, they were married in Spokane, Washington, in 1930.

As Julian stood by the door of his house, studying the street, he thought of the white man. He could not comprehend that a people who had so much would do this to a people who had so little. He understood that the Colville Confederated Tribes was made up of twelve separate tribes that had been forced to live on a common parcel of land. Everything had been taken from the Sin-Aikst, who now lived in Inchelium. Even their tribal name had been taken, leaving them with only their pride. He knew that this land along the Swah net ka was nothing more than a restrictive area where Indians could be kept isolated from others. The whites placed no material value on the reservation land; therefore, they allowed Indians to live on it.

Julian remembered leaving the Philippines when he was a boy of seventeen. He recalled the prejudice and deprivation he faced once he arrived in this country. He could not speak English, but he was fluent in Spanish and Tagalog, one of the languages of the Philippines. He thought of the many restrictions that whites in Seattle had placed upon people like him. Julian's thoughts warmed when memories of his people, his comrades, came back to him. He and the rest of his people found comfort by sticking together and enduring those hard times in Seattle's Chinatown, where they lived.

That was nothing compared to what his Indian friends faced here. He knew he was a part of it now. Julian withdrew his pipe from the windowsill, filled it with tobacco, and lit it. When he returned, he sat down at the table across from Mary and smoked thoughtfully, remembering those past years. They seemed so distant.

Mary's primary concern was for her young children, Lawney and Luana. Her son was now three years old, and her daughter was one. She was aware that she and Julian were going to have to find some work soon or they wouldn't have anything to eat. Mary watched her young children playing on the floor with their dog, Pickles. She was the first to broach the idea of moving to another place, a place where things were happening, even Grand Coulee. They might consider setting up some type of business, perhaps a small restaurant. They could handle that, if they put their minds to it. Julian listened closely to Mary and marveled at her positive attitude. He knew that she was always open to change and always determined.

Julian set his pipe aside in an ashtray and thought of the problems that faced them now. Mary's idea had possibilities. It looked as though Grand Coulee would be a thriving community for the next few years, maybe even longer, depending on how much time it would take to build the dam. There should be a lot of people moving there now. He agreed, in his mind, that they should consider making the move. They might set up a small coffee shop where they could serve sandwiches and homemade pies. Mary enjoyed baking, and Julian knew her pies would be a success anywhere. As he thought, he realized that she was also very good at making fry bread and donuts.

Julian was surprised when Mary stood up, rolled a smoke, and then suggested a business much different from the one in his thoughts. A Chinese restaurant. He tried to mask his surprise as he pondered the idea. He didn't know the first thing about preparing Chinese food. Did she? Did she know anything about Chinese dishes?

Mary folded her arms and firmly stated that they could learn. She didn't think it would be too hard to understand the methods of cooking Chinese food. She reminded Julian of the Chinese restaurant in Spokane where they had enjoyed a meal after their wedding. The dishes were delicious and seemed simple enough to make. They could do it if they tried.

Julian thought a while and shrugged. He had learned not to argue with Mary once she made up her mind. It was not worth the effort. And her idea just might have possibilities. He was fully aware they would have to make a decision soon.

The children sat quietly nearby and listened as their parents talked. They sensed that the conversation dealt with something very important but could not fathom how important. Both could tell that their parents were worried. Pickles, their black and white Boston terrier, sat near them, listening. His large round eyes looked concerned, and his small pointed ears were ever alert.

As the days went by, there were more meetings at the General Store. No one could think of a solution that would relieve the concerns of the people in town. Life went on as usual, but everyone was worried. Men and boys fished for the mountain trout at Hall Creek. Others went farther north to fish at Barnaby Creek. Some traveled to Twin Lakes to catch the large rainbow.

Later in the year, in mid-October, fishermen at Kettle Falls noticed fewer salmon jumping the falls. Over the years, commercial fishing by the whites at Astoria had made the salmon runs smaller, but there were even fewer now. They tried not to think that the salmon runs might be ending. They had not expected it so soon. They had not reasoned that the runs would end so quickly because of the building of a dam.

Some spent hours, then days, watching and hoping to see more salmon. At the time, they did not realize that steel and concrete had been placed on the bedrock at Grand Coulee Dam. They were unaware that the white man had trapped thousands of salmon at Rock Island Dam and were depositing them elsewhere. The Indians did not know that a large hatchery had been built close to Leavenworth, Washington, to make up for some of the salmon that usually went upriver past the construction site of the dam.

The Sin-Aikst and the Swhy al puh would eventually learn that the migration of salmon was going to be stopped forever. Before 1935, the Sin-Aikst and the Swhy al puh who lived in Inchelium could not have guessed the destruction that would come to the salmon, the land, the lives, and, finally, the culture of the people in Inchelium. They could not understand or accept that a culture, centuries old, would no longer exist. Although much thought and talk centered on their approaching problems, no one could think of any solutions. Everyone came to understand that Florence Quill's protests had failed to change the thinking of the white men, who were the cause of their problems. Many now accepted that no one would or could help them. The tribes and their customs would soon be replaced by a way of life foreign to their traditions.

As the salmon fell to lower levels in the Swah net ka, life became very difficult in the Inchelium area. Hunting became the principal way of putting food on the table. Because there was little money, everyone had to ration food and supplies. Greater amounts of camas, bitterroot, and other edible roots were harvested and prepared for later use. Huckleberries, serviceberries, and chokecherries were picked, dried, and stored in larger quantities. Families who had access to good soil began to grow small crops like potatoes, corn, and other vegetables. Others paid what they could afford or bartered possessions and services for whatever vegetables they could get.

Hunters began to worry about the cost of ammunition. Those who used the 30.30 went to smaller caliber rifles, like the 25.20 and, finally, the .22, to cut down on costs. It became necessary to kill with the first shot. Those who were accustomed to enjoyable hunts in the past, many times with others in a party, now hunted alone. It was serious business, a matter of survival, and no longer a pastime.

Mary's concern for the welfare of her family grew daily. More than anything, she worried about not having enough food to feed her children. To think clearly, she walked along the banks of the Swah net ka and tried to reach a decision on what the family should do next. She always took the children with her on her walks. Pickles trotted along before them. Lawney enjoyed the walks when the family was together. He managed to find rocks to throw into the Swah net ka. He had seen others throw rocks and make them skip along the surface of the water. He tried, with some success, to do the same. Sometimes, he found a tree limb and threw it into the Swah net ka, and Pickles swam out to fetch it.

This play always brought laughter from Luana. She would search for sticks and throw them as best she could, imitating her brother. The only other activity on the Swah net ka came from the ferry transporting cars and passengers to and from Gifford. On the other side was white man's land. The eastern boundary of the Colville Reservation was the Swah net ka itself.

During her walks, Mary was plagued by thoughts of not having an education. She felt that if she had been given the chance, she would have done well in school. Mary was determined to somehow make up for her lost years. She was still young and inexperienced, and she often wished her parents were still alive to give her advice.

Her mother, Teresa, had died of pneumonia at Castlegar, B.C., when Mary was only six. Her father, Alex Christian (White Grizzly Bear), cared for her after her mother's death. Because Alex lived off the land, he fished and hunted for a living. He and Mary were constantly moving from one place to another, in search of fish and game. Most of the time, the two lived in a canvas shelter set up along the Swah net ka. Alex and his daughter did not stay in one place long enough for her to attend school.

Later, her father became very ill with tuberculosis while visiting in Omak in 1924. The illness had bothered him for some time, but he had tried to ignore it. During those days in Omak, Alex fought for his life, and near the end of the year, he lost the battle. He was only forty-five years old. Mary was eleven.

For the only time in her life, Mary was able to attend school while she lived in Omak with her foster parents, Charlie and Eliza Hall. But her schooling ended abruptly after two years when the Halls moved to Inchelium. They were now elderly and not in the best of health. She had to be with them constantly, to care for them. Mary thought of these things as she walked with her children along the Swah net ka.

Ever since she was a young girl, Mary had dreamed of having a business. She had no experience or training, but she had a strong desire to create something of her own. Mary thought this was the only way she could make up for her lack of education. She reasoned that the time had come to try. Julian was having a difficult time finding jobs, and they were living from day to day with no long-term plans. The future did not seem bright.

The more she thought about it, the more she felt that Grand Coulee would be the place to start a business. She could not dismiss the idea that she had put forth earlier. Many people were already looking for jobs linked to the construction of the dam. Any business would have a chance of making it, with so many potential customers. She could not think of a better place to gamble.

On some walks, Mary's friend Edo Quill accompanied her. They spent time talking about the problems that Inchelium would face in the near future. They shared their concerns about the time when their small town would no longer exist. As they talked, they exhausted every possibility trying to find ways of solving the problems they would soon face. After hours of walking and talking along the Swah net ka, realizing there were no immediate answers, they would return with the children and Pickles to the General Store to see if there was any more news about the dam.

One day, as Mary and Edo walked along the river, Mary shared her plans: she and Julian had talked about opening a Chinese restaurant in Grand Coulee.

Edo was taken by surprise. She laughed out loud. She was unsure if she had heard Mary right. Was this a joke of some kind? She knew that neither Mary nor Julian knew anything about cooking Chinese food. She also knew that Mary and Julian had little money. Edo was full of questions about this unexpected news.

Mary sat down on a large rock and withdrew a small sack of tobacco from her coat pocket along with a pack of paper. Adeptly, she rolled a smoke, lit it, and inhaled. As she blew smoke into the air, she laughed. She had done a lot of thinking and was confident

Jerome, Edo, and Florence Quill at Inchelium, 1941. Courtesy Teresa Wong.

that she had the answers. She and Julian had eaten Chinese food once in Spokane. The food was so good. She had never tasted anything like it before. She thought that, with some practice, they could learn to cook it. Mary believed it would be worth a try. Besides, what did they have to lose?

Edo shook her head. She could see Julian and Mary getting in over their heads. She was convinced that it would take a lot of money and effort on their part. She knew that once they started, they would always have to be there to run the business. Edo paused, deep in thought. She tried to convince Mary that running a restaurant was a never-ending job. It would be hard work, and they would have to be determined.

Mary smiled. She then invited Edo, when everything was set up, to come over to Grand Coulee and help wait on tables and wash the dishes when she found the time. Edo just laughed.

Julian spent most of his time working at odd jobs. He would take any job that he could find. One day, he got a job digging irrigation ditches for a farmer at the outskirts of Inchelium, along the Swah net ka. The job lasted only a few weeks. Most of the time, he looked for fallen pine trees in the forests around the town, sawed the trees into blocks, and split them into firewood to sell to anyone who needed wood. Sometimes, he helped ranchers put up barbed wire fences to corral their livestock. At other times, he bootlegged whiskey and sold it at a small profit to his Indian friends who could afford it. When people could not afford to pay with money, Julian accepted commodities as payment for his efforts.

When the family was home at the end of the day, Mary prepared supper. Almost all of the food came from the U.S. government in the form of commodities, which she got at the subagency south of town. The government provided staples like beans, flour, cornmeal, oatmeal, powdered milk, salt, and sugar. Mary always carefully rationed the staples. No food was ever wasted. After supper, when the children had been put to bed, Julian and Mary talked and tried to plan what they would do next. As one day passed into another, little changed.

One evening, they were especially worried. The cold weather was moving in, and Julian knew that jobs would be harder to find. He had been lucky to find work the last few months, but it would get harder when the snow fell. They were going to have to find another way soon.

Inwardly, Julian and Mary came to the same conclusion. They were going to have to try something new. If they rationed the food they had, they might be able to make it through the winter. But when spring came, they should make their move to Grand Coulee to see about setting up the restaurant. If they started small, they might have enough cash to get started. If they were lucky, they might make a go of it.

From that time onward, Mary put the family on an even tighter budget. She saved every spare dollar Julian made. Each meal was made even more frugally. At the end of November, just before the snow fell, the family moved to Twin Lakes. Julian knew he would be able to fish through the ice and catch the large rainbow for food. He set up a tent and put in a small flat-topped, wood-burning stove to keep everyone warm. The flat top allowed for cooking.

At Christmastime, Mary and Julian went without presents. The children received gifts that Mary had made on her sewing machine earlier in the year: a shirt for Lawney and a simple dress for Luana. The family stayed at Twin Lakes and endured the winter. The snowfall that winter was heavy, and it was very cold. They spent most of their time inside the tent; Mary kept the heater burning day and night. During the daylight hours, she and Lawney went into the surrounding forest to search for dead tree limbs, which they dragged back to the tent and chopped up for firewood.

Nearly all of the protein they consumed came from the rainbow Julian caught through the ice. Fresh milk was not available, so Mary mixed canned milk with water and gave it to the children. Life that winter was cold and difficult. They returned to their small house in Inchelium in early March, relieved that they had been able to survive the unusually cold winter. After the roads were cleared of snow, they prepared to move to Grand Coulee.

One morning, Dewey Hall and Moops Quill stopped by. Mary had just fed the children a breakfast of mush with canned milk and wild honey. She scraped the leftovers into Pickles's dish. Pickles wagged his stubby tail, anxiously awaiting his meal, and then gulped down the mush. Mary told the children to go outside and play with Pickles, while she and Julian had coffee with their guests.

Mary poured them each coffee, and the four sat around the table quietly talking. Dewey and Moops filled them in on what had been discussed at the last few town hall meetings. They all agreed that no one had any new ideas or solutions regarding the welfare of the people in Inchelium when the time came to move.

Dewey finished his coffee and took his cup to the kitchen. A lot of houses couldn't be moved. Most were too old and not in the best of shape. Dewey didn't know what the people who lived in those houses were going to do.

Julian tamped his pipe with tobacco and lit it as he pondered the situation. Those people would have to live in tents or tepees; there was no other way. He felt certain that their house was strong enough to be moved, but he didn't know how it would be done. They were going to need help when the time came. Right now, they had more pressing problems. He surprised Dewey and Moops with the news that Mary, he, and the children would be moving to Grand Coulee in a week or two. They were going to look into opening a restaurant there. If it couldn't be done, he might be able to find work at the dam.

At the end of February, after the snow on the pass at Gold Mountain had cleared and the road was dry enough to drive safely, the family prepared to leave for the Grand Coulee. Dewey appeared with a battered suitcase and asked if he could join them. He looked a little battered himself, and older than his twenty-seven years, as he came in the door. He was still hung over from the previous night. Dewey and a number of friends had gotten a half-breed to drive to Daisy to buy some beer. It had always been a habit of the locals to get someone who could pass for white to go north to Daisy to buy beer and bring it back. The amount of beer purchased depended on how much money could be collected from everyone who planned to attend the celebration.

The night before, a big party had been planned in Dewey's honor. The party was held to wish him luck in finding a job at Grand Coulee and in staying sober long enough to work at it. Friends gathered along the shore of the Swah net ka. The next day, some of the crowd, who had drunk too much the night before, were found wrapped in blankets, still sleeping it off.

Before they left, during the first week of March, Mary talked to neighbors, letting them know that the family would be gone for a while. They promised to keep an eye on the little house while the family was away. Mary's friends wished them luck in their new venture.

It was late afternoon when everything was packed and the family was ready to go. The children crawled into the back of the Model T, and Dewey, a bit sluggish from drinking too much the night before, struggled to follow them, carrying his suitcase. Pickles anxiously jumped in after him, wagging his stubby tail. After everyone was seated, Julian adjusted the spark and gas levers behind the steering wheel and cranked the Model T. It sputtered and started with a roar.

Before he seated himself behind the wheel of the car, Julian withdrew a small can of Copenhagen from his shirt pocket and stuffed a pinch behind his bottom lip. They traveled up the dirt road to Twin Lakes.

When they reached the lakes, Julian got out and filled a water bag from a spring off to the side of the road. He hung it at its usual place, on the crank insert below the radiator. Julian always did this because, as he drove, the wind hit the bag and kept the water fresh and cool. They continued at a snail's pace, finally reaching the summit of Gold Mountain, at 4,500 feet, where they stopped so that Dewey could relieve himself of some of the beer he'd drunk the night before.

The Model T descended the Gold Mountain grade to Bridge Creek. Julian stopped again so the children could watch the trout swimming below in the San Poil River. Lawney and Luana enjoyed traveling in the Model T, and this was their first trip away from home. They looked forward to new adventures with Pickles always by their side.

Julian spit out his snoose and washed his mouth out with water from the bag. After everyone had returned to the Model T, he drove south four miles, turned west, and climbed another grade at Cashe Creek. A half hour later, they reached the final summit before driving into open country and on to the Nespelem Valley. Julian estimated their arrival time at less than an hour.

As the miles between Inchelium and their new destination diminished, Julian and Mary each thought about leaving Inchelium. They tried to anticipate what the future held for them. Both were concerned about making it in a place away from their home and friends.

As the sun was setting, the Model T arrived at the east side of the Swah net ka. Julian parked off the road, high on a hill overlooking the Grand Coulee Dam construction site. Pickles jumped out and ran to several sagebrush bushes. He sniffed a number of them and proceeded to mark territory.

They all got out and stretched their legs and then walked to the edge of the hill and studied the activity below. Within minutes, hundreds of lights flashed on, and the encroaching darkness was turned into day. The enormous construction site held them in awe. Huge machines of many shapes were moving great amounts of debris and soil. A long belt transported a mixture of rocks and gravel up the river. Thousands of men scurried about attending to a variety of tasks. Ear-splitting explosions rocked the area below. Huge dust clouds mushroomed after dynamite blasted away great rock cliffs across the river. The noise of construction was never ending.

Grand Coulee Dam construction site at night, mid-1930s, showing a view of the catwalk near the upper left corner. Courtesy University of Washington Libraries.

At first, they all stood fascinated by what they saw, but then they were disturbed and saddened as they watched huge machines and powerful explosions tear and blow apart the beautiful landscape before them. Over the years, they had learned from their culture to love the land and treat it with respect. What they were witnessing now was foreign to them. They had not expected this. The wounding and changing of the greatest living being, Mother Earth, was unthinkable to them.

As their eyes continued to survey the scene below, they came to focus on a most unusual spectacle. It was a long, narrow suspension bridge over the river with dozens of men making their way across it. It looked alive as it swayed forcefully from side to side.

"Dad, where are those people going?" Lawney asked.

"They're probably going up to that place called B Street," Dewey answered. "That's where your dad and I are going in the morning. Right, Julian?"

After watching what appeared to be mayhem below, Julian and Dewey set up a tent borrowed from a neighbor in Inchelium. This would be their home until they were settled in Grand Coulee. Mary prepared baloney sandwiches for everyone. Water to wash down the meal would come from the bag Julian had hung on the crankshaft of the Model T.

That night, everyone tried to sleep in the small tent overlooking the huge construction site. It was difficult because of the constant noise generated by the many machines below. Dewey's snoring did not help matters. And, of course, there was the excitement of knowing that, in the early morning, Julian and Dewey would cross the bridge, drive up the hill to Grand Coulee, and search for B Street and a new life.

4

B STREET

Entrepreneurs began arriving in Grand Coulee even before construction of the dam was approved in 1933. Most came from different parts of the state of Washington. Their goal was to set up businesses to cater to the thousands of men they knew would be moving into the area to work on the dam. They reasoned that the vacant sloping hillside and the bench above, covered by sagebrush and tumbleweed, would serve their needs. The town of Grand Coulee had the land surveyed and divided into lots along both sides of a street. The entrepreneurs purchased the lots, which they leased to those who wanted to start small businesses. They thought it was a good idea to have the lots at a distance from the small town of Grand Coulee itself. In time, the town's residents would come to resent the behavior, noise, and distractions generated by those who frequented these establishments.

As men arrived, the number of small businesses grew. The first was a restaurant run by Mrs. A. E. "Johnny" Johnson and Mrs. B. G. Raymond. Men had asked the two women to prepare meals for them. Mrs. Johnson and Mrs. Raymond served the meals on a makeshift table constructed from loose boards and sawhorses, outside the tent where they lived and cooked. The business was eventually called the Grand Coulee Café.

In those early days, building regulations were not enforced, and almost all of the new buildings were poorly constructed. Most owners of the small businesses knew nothing of construction or even carpentry, but this did not hold them back. Friends or family members sometimes pitched in to help as they fought the clock to get the structures up. Most of the buildings barely kept the weather out. There were cracks in the walls, and windows were not set properly. Dust penetrated to the interiors during severe windstorms, causing all kinds of havoc. The buildings were raised quickly and with no regard for design or comfort. Nearly all of the structures were made of rough lumber and tarpaper. Some were painted later.

Many business owners cared only about putting up an enclosure, a place where they could make money by selling something. This assembly of poorly constructed buildings on both sides of the dusty thoroughfare became known as B Street, or, familiarly, "The Street."

Before 1934, there was no power in the area, and people used kerosene and gas lamps for light. The early businesses had to get along with this type of lighting. Water came from wells that were dug here and there or, in some cases, it was purchased from entrepreneurs who transported it on trucks in large steel tanks. Ice had to be delivered to The Street, and cakes of it were carried by hand to businesses that needed it. When electricity was connected, more businesses began to appear along B Street. There were grocery stores, restaurants, drug stores, barbershops, hardware stores, bars, taverns, dry cleaners, small hotels, and even a small movie theater and a bowling alley. A number of businesses built a second floor, with sleeping rooms for the prostitutes who would serve the thousands of workingmen and later visitors who were curious about women other than their wives.

Luckily, the price of goods was reasonable on B Street. A loaf of bread cost nine cents, and eggs were fifteen cents per dozen. Coffee sold for twenty-five to thirty cents per pound, while the price of two cans of milk was fifteen cents. A box of cornflakes cost fifteen cents. Bacon sold for fifteen cents per pound. The prices were comparable to those in nearby towns such as Almira, Nespelem, and Wilbur.

Beer was the most popular drink on The Street. It cost ten cents a glass. Some taverns charged only five cents a glass, but people who drank it thought it was watered down. Occasionally, there were shortages of water, but the workingmen paid no attention to this because they preferred their beer. When certain places closed at 2:00 A.M., workingmen could go upstairs and pay twenty-five cents a glass for moonshine. Sometimes they enjoyed the company of the ladies of the night who were up there waiting for them.

On Friday night, B Street was especially active. Friday was payday. The noise was sometimes deafening as taverns and dance halls turned up the loudspeakers playing music from records to attract the workingmen who passed by on the boardwalks.

As the numbers of people on B Street swelled, problems arose. There had never been enough money to build a storm drain and sewer system for The Street, so the waste was channeled to Rattlesnake Canyon. The smell drifted everywhere, and there was no escaping it. People with a sense of humor called the place "Poop Lagoon." To others, it was not so funny. Nature, however, was considerate, and the shifting winds distributed the smell generously to everyone in the area. It was an inescapable problem that everyone had to endure.

The families who had come to Electric City, Grand Coulee, Mason City, and other small communities nearby looked down on B Street. They did their best to avoid any association with it. Sometimes, articles in the local papers denounced the lewd activities that took place there. Richard Neuberger, in his book *The Promised Land*, declares that "sin and salvation were doing business at the same time in the piano box town of B Street." As time went on, the upstanding citizens realized that they had no power to change things. The chief of police, a man by the name of McGinn, cast a blind eye on everything that happened on B Street. Raids proved to be funny and ineffective. While the upright citizens of Grand Coulee remained indignant about The Street, the workingmen and ladies of the night who played there enjoyed life, as usual.

During the summer, the temperature rose, and it got very hot on B Street. The buildings had no air conditioning, and people sometimes used electric fans to cool off. To add to the discomfort, windstorms brought unbelievable amounts of dust. Residents could see the storms coming up the coulee, stirring huge clouds, and braced for the onslaught. They filled the cracks in the walls of the poorly constructed buildings with paper, cloth, and anything pliable, hoping to prevent dust from getting inside. In spite of their efforts, great amounts of dust managed to penetrate and cover everything. Brooms and dustpans had to be used to remove the dust. Sometimes, the dust was so thick that it was difficult to see across the street.

When snow piled up everywhere in the winter, it was difficult to maneuver automobiles. The slippery roads were covered with gravel so that cars of all sorts could travel without getting stuck. However, the snow added beauty to B Street. The buildings took on a different character, and discrepancies of design disappeared beneath the snow. The street appeared innocent and quaint, like a

Christmas card illustration of a peaceful hamlet during the Holy Season. The interiors of the taverns and dancehalls were cleaner, without the mud and dust of other seasons, since the boardwalks and streets were covered with hard-packed snow. Cigarette butts that usually lay in the hundreds on the floors next to the bars were dutifully swept up to honor the Holy Season.

Colorful Christmas lights sparkled through the falling snowflakes, and B Street actually became beautiful. Business owners who were sensitive to the season played Christmas carols on their record players instead of the usual raucous music designed to entice customers. Nearly every business put up Christmas trees of various sizes. The atmosphere of the Holy Season affected everyone. Some who lived elsewhere in Washington went home for the holidays, but most, who came from out of state, remained at The Street. Everyone celebrated the season by indulging in more drinking. The only activity that experienced a downturn was fighting between the workingmen, who appeared to be less combative during the holiest of seasons.

During the spring, B Street took on a totally different character. The rains quickly melted the snow, and the roads became muddy. It was next to impossible to get across. Cars trying to negotiate B Street were mired in very deep mud. Everyone referred to the mud as "gumbo." It was everywhere. An enterprising man who understood the problem brought in a tractor and parked it near B Street. When cars or trucks became stuck in the mud, he brought in his tractor and pulled them out for five dollars.

Jean Nicholson, a local historian, shared an amusing story about the muddy conditions of B Street: "One day, a man walking the sidewalk spied a hat sitting on top of the mud on B Street. He thought that it was a nice hat, so he carefully made his way onto the street to retrieve it. When he picked it up, he saw a man's head under it. The head looked up and advised, 'Think nothing of it.

Front of Grand Coulee Club with three contractors, late 1930s.
Courtesy Dennis King Photography.

There is a wagon of hay under me and two horses. Can you help get us out?'"

The muddy conditions were extremely difficult. People tracked the mud everywhere. Dance hall owners had to hire workers to stand by and shovel the mud off the floors so that dancers could enjoy themselves. Walking across B Street was also difficult. At times, pedestrians lost their galoshes or boots as they tried to cross the street, and people often sank up to their knees in the mud.

(Opposite) *Looking south on B Street during the winter of 1936, showing Swanee Rooms* (top), *and looking north on B Street during the winter of 1938, showing Atwater Drugs* (bottom). *Courtesy Dennis King Photography.*

Everyone was happy when the rain finally stopped, and warmer weather came.

All who came to B Street had suffered from the Depression and were relieved to find employment and escape the poverty they had been facing. They worked hard, and they played hard. The Street became a home away from home for many lonely workingmen and women striving to make their way during the thirties.

5

WORKING STIFFS

When the nation received the news that a large dam was to be constructed at Grand Coulee, hundreds, then thousands, of young men from across the country journeyed there seeking employment. The Depression had hurt nearly everyone, and people were hungry and destitute. Men from the state of Washington were given preference in hiring. After the state quotas had been satisfied, people from out of state were hired. Many walked, hopped the rail, or hitchhiked with few belongings and little money in their pockets.

When they arrived, most had to live in the meanest of shelters. Those who were fortunate enough to have cars lived in them. Others pooled their money and purchased canvas tents as shelter against the extremes of the weather. Some simply lived in caves they had dug into the hillsides, using burlap bags to cover the openings. Others obtained large crates of wood that had been used to ship merchandise such as pianos, modified them, and set them up around the B Street area. Those early months of 1933 proved to be very difficult for all who came to work on the dam.

Before construction began, a number of people who lived near the river in shacks and tents were forced to move to make way for the initial preparation of the dam site. One of these was Ferd Warner, who ran a barbershop. His place was so small that the barber had to step outside just to strop his razor. Men who wanted a haircut or a shave had to stand in line outside and wait their turn. During the cold and rainy seasons, this became very difficult for the customers, but Ferd boasted the cheapest haircuts in town, and his customers endured it. When the day came to move, Ferd simply loaded the shack onto a truck and relocated his business, which quickly thrived as the working stiffs began to arrive in greater numbers.

Initially, the men constructed cofferdams out of steel sheet pilings. The cofferdams directed the river away from sections of the bedrock so that a foundation could be prepared to hold the great weight of the dam. The engineers demanded that the bedrock be solid and watertight. The men found this work painstaking but knew it had to be done. Once the cofferdams were completed, the workers cleared the overburden (rock and soil) from the solid granite base, which was then reinforced with a special grout. Hundreds of holes were drilled into the rock, and the grout was forced in with high-pressure pumps. After one section had been prepared, the men drove in new cofferdams to direct the river away from other sections.

After the bedrock was prepared, other workmen constructed forms for holding specially prepared concrete. The House of Magic, located near the dam site, tested the concrete before it was poured. Many considered this work desirable because they learned more about the special concrete, and it also proved to be one of the safer jobs at the site.

The pouring of concrete was continuous and timed to the minute. Cool water flowing through pipes inserted in the concrete controlled the drying process. After allowing seventy-two hours for

House of Magic, the concrete-mixing plant at the dam site, around 1938. Courtesy University of Washington Libraries.

curing, workers scrubbed the concrete blocks with wire brushes in order to ensure a perfect fit with the new blocks that were poured into forms on top of them. This procedure required the efforts of several engineers and hundreds of working stiffs.

Contrary to popular belief, no worker was ever buried alive in the concrete. The pouring of concrete into blocks did not allow that. Men were injured or killed because rocks, steel equipment, or tools fell on them. A few fell from the high cliffs on the west side as they worked the jackhammers. Others were maimed or killed when they were run over by heavy equipment.

As work continued on the base of the dam, jackhammer operators and powder monkeys (men who planted explosives) prepared the rock cliffs on the west side of the river. The powder monkeys inserted dynamite into the newly drilled holes, and the excess rock and related material were blown away so that the rock could be solidly joined with the concrete and steel of the dam. This was painstaking and dangerous work, and many men were hurt when miscalculations resulted in unexpectedly powerful explosions.

Other men built the steel supports that would help anchor the concrete as it was poured. Welding and riveting were continuous as the work progressed. Only the most skilled and experienced workingmen were chosen for this part of the construction. Those who tossed the white-hot rivets up to the riveters had to be accurate and confident in what they were doing.

Many agreed that the dirtiest job of all was applying CA 5, a substance that made the steel rustproof. It looked like tar, black and sticky. When it dried, it was very hard and stiff. The men who worked with it couldn't wash it off their clothes, which they had to replace every week. The company paid those costs.

The Mason-Walsh-Atkinson and Kier Company (MWAK) constructed a huge mess hall in the Mason City area, across the river, east of Grand Coulee. It served meals to hundreds of men during the heavy construction period of 1935 until the completion of the dam in 1941. MWAK constructed a large number of bunkhouses nearby, row after row, and the building complex resembled a military outpost. The men were grateful because many of them had

Working stiffs scaling cliffs on the west side of the dam site, 1938.
Courtesy Dennis King Photography.

been living in automobiles, tents, and even crates to stay out of the cold. This new construction had showers that everyone could use. It was a welcome relief for those who had been bathing themselves in basins or laundry tubs. Washing machines were installed to make their lives even easier.

Thousands of men were now employed at the dam. Some accommodations provided places not only to sleep but to prepare meals. Most of the shelters had electricity and water. There were often indoor toilets, which the stiffs shared with others and made sure to maintain and keep clean.

As the construction of the dam progressed, the tempo of activity accelerated, and the noise was deafening. From time to time, loud explosions rocked the atmosphere and created huge clouds of dust. The dust was everywhere, sometimes so thick it was hard to see the men as they worked. Hundreds of stiffs moved about, involved in a variety of tasks. They resembled ants scurrying about with no purpose in mind. To the casual observer, there seemed to be no planning or thought in the actions of the working stiffs, but in reality all activity at the construction site was precisely planned. Efforts and accomplishments were always ahead of schedule. This continued until the overall project was completed.

Large machines and equipment moved ponderously in every direction. Some were engaged in excavating, and others were loading great amounts of overburden onto large trucks. Again, the logic behind their constant movement and activity was not obvious. The noise that accompanied the huge machines was deafening.

Chuck Hall, who was with the Bureau of Reclamation at that time, had many humorous stories to share about the adventurous young men employed under him. Most were hard workers and eager to please. They were courageous and took risks to get the job done. The men were innovative and always sought out new ways to perform their work more efficiently.

Conversations between the stiffs were mostly about their everyday jobs or about the women they planned to meet after their shifts were up. They were always appreciative of the attractive women who made B Street their place of business. To the young working-men, B Street was a dream come true, and they enjoyed the time they spent there immensely.

Most of the workingmen were single and wanted something exciting to do when their shifts were up. Others were married but could not afford to bring their wives and families to the Grand Coulee area and were free to do what they wanted in their off hours. This often included a visit to B Street.

When the workers walked The Street, especially when night was falling, they had to watch out for others scuffling. More than once, men would come crashing out of the entrances of the taverns that lined both sides of the street. After beating on each other, they would embrace, shake hands, and return to the taverns for more beer. For many, this was standard operating procedure on B Street.

Later, when the working stiffs wanted to have fun, they went to the larger taverns that had dance halls. In the late afternoon and evening, taxi dancers plied their trade with many a lonely man who had come in for entertainment when his shift was up. The taxi dancers lived in nearby Grand Coulee or up on the Heights above town. Many were married, and some had children. The men enjoyed their company and spent most of their spare time either talking to them or dancing. The women purchased tickets for five cents each and then charged their partners ten cents a dance. Some of the workers considered themselves good dancers and would search out the best-looking dancers. Some noticed that the three- or sometimes five-piece orchestras that performed in the dance halls seemed to play the music faster than it was supposed to be played. This made the song go faster, and it became impossible to finish dancing all the way around the floor for a dime. As the orchestra increased its tempo, the men had difficulty keeping up, and more than once, the ladies reprimanded their partners for stepping on their toes. A number learned that the ultimate goal of the dance hall operators was to make money as quickly as they could. Most of the working stiffs were usually too drunk to realize this and continued to pay the taxi dancers ten cents a dance until they were nearly broke.

The Grand Coulee Club was a favorite among the working stiffs. The dance floor was fairly large, and there were always a number of good-looking taxi dancers available. Most of the taxi dancers made it clear that they were not prostitutes. But they did encourage the men to buy them drinks, as they received a commission on each beverage sold. The men had no way of knowing that their dance partners were being served nothing more than Kool-Aid or some other nonalcoholic concoction.

Days, weeks, and then months went by, and gradually more Indians were seen on B Street. Some had come from Nespelem and the Okanogan Valley. A few of the lighter-skinned Indians had been hired to work on the dam, but the full bloods were usually turned away. Those breeds who got jobs became part of the army of working stiffs that had grown to more than seven thousand. They were accepted on B Street as well and had access to all of the establishments, including the taverns and dance halls. The bartenders cared little if their customers were Indians. They cared only for the profit they would make by selling beer to anyone who could afford it. Most of the Indians stayed at Jim O'Brien's Cabins, where the rent was reasonable. O'Brien accepted them because he was part Indian himself.

Those identified as Indians, especially the ones with darker skins, had more difficulty being accepted on B Street. They were not allowed to drink alcohol in the bars and taverns. These Indian men were not allowed in the halls to dance with the white taxi dancers.

Another problem arose when the newspapers disclosed that more men would be needed to work on the dam. Like everyone else, Negroes came to Grand Coulee to find work, many from the big cities of the West Coast. Needless to say, the Negroes had suffered greatly in the Depression. If whites were having hard times, it is safe to say that Negroes were having harder times. But Negroes who joined the line of whites seeking jobs at the dam site were clearly unwelcome. When the Mason-Walsh-Atkinson and Kier Company hired workers for the dam, the Negroes were always overlooked. It became extremely hard for them to accept this because times were very hard. Wherever they went, they repeatedly faced prejudice.

The Negroes waited patiently to be hired but were ignored over and over again. Paul Pitzer, in his book *Grand Coulee*, tells the story of a Negro man who walked all the way from Seattle to Grand Coulee to find a job. Upon reaching the dam site, he applied for work and was turned down. Although a number of people seemed to know of the man and his situation, U.S. Reemployment officials always claimed ignorance of his case.

Finally, when it became obvious that Negroes would never be hired to fill construction jobs at the dam, the National Association for the Advancement of Colored People (NAACP) came to speak up for them and present their case. In March 1936, representatives of the Urban League met with the government and pointed out that Negroes had not been able to get jobs at the dam. After several meetings, Raymond F. Walter, the acting commissioner of the Bureau of Reclamation, intervened. After lengthy negotiations, MWAK reluctantly hired about fifty Negro men in order to avoid continued protests.

This decision turned out to be a hollow victory for the NAACP because MWAK made sure the Negroes got the lowest-paying jobs. When stiffs were laid off due to lack of work, the Negroes were the first to go. When workers were again in demand, the whites were the first to be rehired. At the job site, Negro laborers were totally ignored by white laborers, who avoided working closely with them. When the water bucket was passed around to the thirsty workers, whites would not drink out of a bucket that had been used by Negroes. The discrimination went on from day to day with no reprieve.

Negroes were not allowed to live in Mason City, where most of the white workers lived in new houses and accommodations constructed by MWAK on the east side of the river. They could live only in a small area on the outskirts of B Street, near Grand Coulee. The whites made it clear that Negroes would not be welcome on The Street. It was reserved for whites, and Negroes did not dare enter.

At this time, Engineers' Town, on the west side of the river, was nearing completion, and the engineers and their families were moving into well-designed houses with manicured lawns. Beech, weeping willow, and white birch trees planted next to evergreens provided adequate shade and a pleasing atmosphere for the residents. Engineers' Town seemed like a paradise compared to the places where the working stiffs lived.

The residents of Engineers' Town did not want drunken workers going through their neighborhood at all hours of the day and night, so the company erected a catwalk near the construction site for the hundreds of working stiffs who lived on the other side of the river. The catwalk, made of wooden planks that were anchored to steel supports and cables, stretched across the river just below the dam. The workingmen used it to get across the river and up to

B Street without going through Engineers' Town. One engineer remembered what a tempting attraction the catwalk became for the children in the area. The young boys loved to sneak out on the structure and rock it until it swayed. They were always caught and shooed away before they injured themselves.

The men who crossed the catwalk had no trouble on their way to B Street, but when they returned after a night of heavy drinking, it was a different story. It was not uncommon for someone to fall and end up in the fast-flowing river below. In fact, there was a watchman, known to be a great swimmer, who was hired to sit in a rowboat directly below the catwalk. It was his job to rescue anyone who fell in.

As time went on, more than seventy-four hundred working stiffs and dozens of Bureau of Reclamation engineers were working at the dam. The construction was constant, with three shifts assigned for eight hours each. The project was so large that most people had to find out about what was going on at other parts of the dam by reading the local newspapers.

The men did not make much money working at the dam, but it was more than any of them had earned in the past. The Depression had left its mark on them, and they were more than happy with their weekly paychecks. Most of them made fifty cents an hour. With overtime, the average paycheck was twenty dollars to twenty-five dollars a week. After they were paid on Friday, most went directly to B Street to have a good time. Before the weekend ended, many were broke and anxiously awaited the next payday.

During the winter of 1935, the weather began to get very cold. On January 31, MWAK stopped all concrete pours, and in early February, the Columbia River froze. One thousand workers lost their

Catwalk, to the left of the larger span, used by workers to access B Street, mid-1930s. Courtesy Dennis King Photography.

jobs. Days later, another thousand were let go. Many who were laid off had to ration food and supplies. They also curtailed their visits to B Street because they could not afford spending money there. The stiffs often preferred to remain in their cabins to read or simply listen to the radio.

The practice of laying off workers started a boom-and-bust cycle that continued through the remainder of the project. The layoffs affected the entire economy of B Street. When the men did not make their nightly rounds to drink and spend time with the women, both the taverns and the women suffered. In March, when the weather warmed, MWAK rehired the workers, and the construction schedule, and activities on B Street, continued on pace.

As construction accelerated, the stiffs experienced heavier

Working stiffs standing in line for paychecks, late 1930s.
Courtesy Dennis King Photography.

workloads. Sometimes, they were too tired to cross the catwalk and make their way up the hill to The Street. Most went directly to their shelters and to bed. Some were too tired to eat and slept through their meals.

On June 13, 1935, the usual B Street activity of chasing women was interrupted when James J. Braddock, the heavyweight prize-fighter, challenged Max Baer for the world championship. Every stiff of Irish descent was glued to a radio in every honky-tonk in town. In those days of the Depression, Braddock, who had risen from hard times and poverty, represented the heart and soul of nearly everyone who had suffered a similar fate. He was their champion.

During the grueling fight, Braddock, who was in better shape than Baer, left-jabbed and then threw combination punches to keep the champion off balance. At the end of fifteen rounds, the judges awarded Braddock the decision, making him the heavyweight champion of the world.

After the fight was over, B Street and the rest of the country went wild. The celebration of Braddock's win continued throughout the evening. Braddock received numerous toasts, and sex was placed on the back burner. For every working stiff, it was a night to remember.

During the next winter, freezing weather once again halted construction, and many workers were laid off for close to two months. Everyone experienced hard economic times once again. But as warmer weather returned, life in the area fell into its usual pattern.

As work on the dam progressed, many of these bright and innovative young men continued to come up with new ways to get their jobs done. This always impressed their superiors and helped keep construction ahead of schedule. These dedicated young men did not know that one day, after December 7, 1941, they would go on to face even greater challenges.

6

PRETTY LADIES

The business of women selling their services to men is nearly as old as humanity itself. Almost every society in the world has experienced this type of behavior at one time or another. Traditionally, upper social circles have reacted with contempt and dismay. Sometimes, laws have been passed in an attempt to control it. Regardless of resistance, this type of behavior has always flourished.

The Great Depression that began in the United States in October 1929 caused an economic nightmare, not only in this country, but throughout the industrialized world. Many people experienced extreme hardships. Some fathers left their families in search of work, never to return, and their wives often took in male boarders who had jobs and could help pay the bills. Many women had to make a variety of humiliating compromises in order to survive from day to day. Those who did not have the strength or the discipline to handle the miseries of their lives turned to alcohol.

Some women resorted to peddling apples on street corners for the better part of the day in order to buy food for their children, hence the term "Apple Annies" came to be. Others turned to shoplifting food for their families. At times, the younger women in the family experimented with amateur prostitution and some eventually learned the tricks of the trade.

The Women's Prison Association (WPA), founded in 1844, was the oldest advocacy group for women in the United States. In early 1930, the directors wrote, "The exigencies of the time [the Great Depression] have brought their added problems to the WPA. Extreme poverty is having its effect upon the groups of women we work with, as well as upon the rest of the community. Shoplifting, by those who have never done it before, now comes more often to our attention. Disaster has come through lack of job openings and, consequently, of self respect."

The WPA was the first to call for the decriminalization of prostitution in the United States. The group believed that the entire nation was facing extremely difficult times and that women engaged in prostitution were only trying to find a way to support themselves.

In 1932, the WPA supported a press release from the League of Women Voters: "We believe that prostitution is a social problem, that it should be treated as such, and that, as soon as practicable, it should be eliminated from the Criminal Code; moreover, that it should be handled with adequate provision for medical, psychiatric and social care."

The Depression drove many attractive women to B Street. When they heard that thousands of workingmen were to be hired for the construction of Grand Coulee Dam, they foresaw new avenues of endeavor for themselves. Dozens came to the small town along the Columbia River with the aim of providing their services to hundreds of workers who would soon be drawing paychecks for the first time in a long while.

Most of these young women came from Seattle, Spokane, and

Tacoma, but others were from all parts of the country. As the number of workingmen increased, the number of women grew. They were drawn to Grand Coulee for one reason: money. More money than they had ever seen in their lives. Some came from good homes, but the Depression had hurt everyone. They had witnessed the suffering of their families, as everyone strove to eke out a meager living. At times, women who were merely passing through stayed a few nights, and many of the stiffs enjoyed the presence of these newcomers. The visitors had a great time and left B Street a little wiser, and also a little richer.

There are still residents of Grand Coulee who remember B Street in its heyday. Everyone seems to agree that most of the women who came to this remote street were honest, caring, and considerate of others.

Two men who as teenagers delivered newspapers on B Street could attest to the kindness of these women. Jack Nicholson remembers cold winter mornings when it was snowing heavily and he was invited into the warmth of a woman's room and handed a cup of hot chocolate. He was delighted to run errands to the local cleaners or the shoe repair shop for the ladies. He knew he would be rewarded with a twenty-five-cent tip, a lot of money for a young boy in those days. Bill Miller, who later worked as an engineer at the construction site, had fond memories of the women who made B Street their home during the thirties. "I remember there were mornings, in the cold of winter, when I would be making my deliveries and one of the women would grab me by the arm and pull me inside her warm apartment and have breakfast waiting for me. I decided, early on, that this was not information I should share with my mother. I was afraid she would make me quit my job."

Jean Nicholson, the local historian of Grand Coulee, had lived in the area most of her life and was knowledgeable about almost everything B Street had to offer. Over the years, she shared her information with others. People were always curious about the women who made their living as prostitutes. Most agreed that prostitution at that time was not the ugly profession it is often made out to be. Instead, it was a necessary occupation when money was hard to come by. The Depression was in full force, and many women were suffering. As historians delved deeper into the subject, they understood that most prostitutes, or pretty ladies, as they came to be known, actually had a strong moral code. The people who came to know them seldom had anything but good things to say about them. A number of Grand Coulee residents even believed that the presence of prostitutes on B Street made their town safer for their own young daughters. They were grateful the women were there.

But now and then, upright citizens of Grand Coulee registered complaints about the lifestyle of the working stiffs and pretty ladies. On one occasion, the Commercial Club sent a resolution to Governor Clarence Martin in Olympia and to Ed Schwellenbach, the Grant County attorney. The resolution characterized the activities on B Street as "vicious nightlife" and decried the "deplorable vice conditions."

In time, the governor appointed a commission to investigate the complaint. The commission met and decided the resolution had grossly exaggerated the situation. The working stiffs and the pretty ladies continued their activities uninterrupted. The only change on The Street was an increase in male tourists, who were completely awed by the number of attractive women.

While a number of residents of Grand Coulee and the Heights looked down their noses at B Street for what they imagined was happening there, they were unaware of the goings-on within their own neighborhoods. In his book *A River Lost*, Blaine Harden tells about the experiences of his father, Arno Harden, during the summer of 1936. After losing his job at an apple-packing shed in Wenatchee, Washington, Arno and his brother, Albert, found work collecting debris and cleaning blocks of concrete at the Grand Coulee Dam construction site. The work was tedious and painstaking, and the wet, cold weather made it somewhat dangerous.

Arno did not like his job and began looking for employment more to his liking. After several weeks, he saw an ad for a milk deliveryman in the local newspaper. He applied, signed a contract, and got the job.

In order to complete his delivery schedule, Harden had to rise early in the morning, at 3:00 A.M. As more people moved into the area, the number of deliveries increased. He found himself on a tight schedule. On one of his deliveries, an attractive young woman greeted him at the door. To his surprise, she was completely nude. She smiled coyly and invited him in. Surprised, and at odds with himself, he thanked her and informed her that he was behind in his deliveries and had to decline the invitation.

As time went on, he encountered other unclothed women in a variety of seductive poses. Upon entering an enclosed porch to make another morning delivery, he saw a very well endowed customer lying completely naked on a recliner next to the kitchen door. Arno had to politely decline the offers made by these attractive women, because he was a happily married man who lived with his family in the Heights. He also felt that he worked hard for his money and did not want to squander a penny of it.

Arno was aware of the feelings of many residents of Grand Coulee and the Heights. It made him smile when he thought about the community leaders who were outspoken in their disapproval of the activities of the pretty ladies on B Street. He surmised that they would be outraged if they learned of the questionable behavior of some of their own neighbors.

After Arno left his job as a milkman, the new milkman was incapable of dismissing or ignoring the young women who were still appearing nude when he made his deliveries. He tried his best to juggle his time between delivering the milk and accommodating the needs of the women, but, alas, within weeks, he was worn out and quit the job.

Two types of establishments on B Street offered the services of women: those with class and those without. The Red Rooster fell into the latter category. When male tourists came to see what was going on, the pretty ladies at the Red Rooster often greeted them. They could be seen leaning out of the second-floor windows, displaying their attributes and encouraging every male who could hear or see them to come up and have a good time. They became known as the Yoo Hoo Girls. Many were very attractive, and potential customers frequently took them up on their offers.

Every person with an interest soon knew where to find the houses of prostitution: the Pioneer, Grace's Model Rooms, the Red Rooster, the Frontier, the Big 4, Seattle Rooms, and Swanee Rooms. Most of these places had small rooms upstairs where business took place. Other establishments had no names and were simply called "rooming houses," but everyone knew their trade. A few of the establishments were exclusive, and a customer had to be known to enter the premises. The men spent an average of twenty minutes with the pretty ladies, at the cost of two dollars a visit.

Occasionally, pimps showed up on B Street, but mostly they were not involved with the pretty ladies. The working stiffs dealt with the ladies directly. In reality, B Street was not a safe place for pimps who might be overly assertive. The stiffs were a rough and ready bunch and did not take kindly to interference when it came to their dealings with women. Because of this, the pimps stayed as far away as possible from the fun-loving, rowdy, and hard-drinking working stiffs.

Over the years, some workingmen found pleasure in the company of individual women. They became devoted and loyal to the women they had come to know and care about. These men developed steadfast friendships during their time on The Street. For a few, these relationships were just as important as sex.

The town of Grand Coulee tried to maintain control over the health of everyone involved and required that each pretty lady get a weekly checkup for venereal disease. A few cases were diagnosed, and those affected took time off until they were cured.

When the police wanted to fill their coffers, they conducted a raid. They generally did this on a monthly basis, just for the money. The officers would choose certain houses on B Street, round up a number of the ladies, bring them to the police station in Grand Coulee, and book them. Within minutes, the madam appeared to bail them out, and they'd be back at work within the hour, often before the police had completed their paperwork. In truth, the raids were nothing more than an opportunity for the police department to increase its revenue. There was some excitement when the raids took place, but everyone knew about the police procedures and did not take them seriously. Policemen rarely patrolled B Street and were seldom called in to handle disputes. If problems did arise, they were generally settled without the help of the police department.

During their free time, the pretty ladies enjoyed some diversions of their own in the vicinity of the small town of Grand Coulee. One of their favorite Sunday excursions was a trip to Soap Lake. They enjoyed traveling on the newly constructed Speedball Highway. They marveled at the splendor of the huge rock cliffs that lined both sides of the Grand Coulee and appreciated the quiet beauty the coulee afforded them along the way. At Soap Lake, they would soak in the warm water for hours. The Indians believed the water had healing powers, and many of the ladies came to believe this legend. They loved getting away from the hustle and bustle of B Street whenever they could.

If they were able to hitch a ride or pay someone to drive them, they would head to Owhi Lake, on the Colville Reservation, traveling on the dusty graveled road between Grand Coulee and Nespelem. As they passed through Nespelem, they stared with great interest at the Indian residents. Many of the women had never been on an Indian reservation. The Indians usually looked upon the pretty ladies with indifference. Once they reached their destination, the ladies swam and picnicked for hours, enjoying the sights and the solitude of the beautiful lake. They watched Indian fishermen sitting quietly in rowboats, hoping to catch a few eastern brook trout. Dry Falls was another favorite destination. There, the pretty ladies hiked deep into the canyons and savored the beauty and privacy of the lake below.

On warm sunny days, some of the pretty ladies walked down to the hills' edge overlooking the dam site and watched the men at work. They were awed by the magnitude of the project and the noise that it generated as huge machines and thousands of stiffs performed their work. Sometimes they could see the men they had entertained the night before working on projects below.

The radio was a favorite diversion for the pretty ladies. Some of the best singers and big bands performed in the 1930s: Tommy and Jimmy Dorsey, Artie Shaw, Benny Goodman, and Bob Crosby. Great singers like Bea Wain, Maxine Grey, and Bing Crosby became favorites. Tex Beneke, from the great Glenn Miller band, could not only sing but play the saxophone as well. It was the time when the best music in America was being composed, and everyone loved it. If the women were not working during the early evening hours, they enjoyed the popular music of the day and radio programs that featured Amos and Andy, Fibber McGee and Molly, and Jack Benny, as well as *I Love a Mystery*.

At other times, after a little too much drinking, some pretty ladies discussed their work on The Street. They often shared intimacies laced with ribaldry. With gleeful merriment, a few discussed the natural attributes of some clients or the woeful shortcomings of others. Their friendships were strong. They were a close-knit group and always looked out for one another.

When the Grand Coulee Theatre, located near B Street, showed a new movie, there would always be a group of pretty ladies in the front row sharing popcorn. It often seemed to others that they behaved like adolescent girls. Watching movies became a welcome escape for many of the pretty ladies.

Bill Miller remembered his teenage days when he worked at the Grand Coulee Theatre as a janitor for a dollar a week. "The children of Grand Coulee were not allowed to attend a movie in this theater because it was in close proximity to B Street," Bill reminisced. "The theater was so poorly constructed that people who couldn't afford a dime for admission would view the movie from outside the theater through cracks in the walls.

"I remember when the new Roosevelt Theatre opened in Grand Coulee, I received a phone call from Mickey Knox, the manager at the time. He offered me a job for three dollars and fifty cents a week. I thought that was big money. Then when Ollie Hartman took over as manager, he offered me six dollars a week. That was a lot of money for a young man in those days."

The Roosevelt Theatre during the late 1930s.
Courtesy Dennis King Photography.

Eventually, the pretty ladies went across Midway Avenue to enjoy a movie. The Roosevelt Theater had opened for business and showed first-run movies. Rod Hartman, whose father was the manager of the theater, had vivid memories of those days. "The building was constructed much better than the Grand Coulee Theater, and it housed 750 people. The movies were the best Hollywood had to offer. The cost of admission was higher than at the Grand Coulee, but a ticket had a lot to offer the moviegoer, especially on Wednesday

(Opposite) *Silver Dollar Club, with owner Whitey Shannon (wearing bow tie), the bartender, and customers* (top), *and with a pretty lady and working stiffs, 1938* (bottom). *Courtesy Dennis King Photography.*

and Thursday evenings. The payroll department didn't issue its cash envelopes to workers until Friday, so midweek was a slow time for business, and the management of the Roosevelt had to find ways to entice customers.

"Wednesday night was not just a movie, it was an event sometimes lasting from 7:00 to 11:00 P.M. It became known as Bank Night. First, there was a raffle. A numbered stub would be handed out each time an admission ticket was purchased during the week. On Wednesday, a number would be drawn, and a customer who could produce the corresponding stub would win a good sum of cash, sometimes as much as three hundred dollars. The winner had to be present. If no one produced the winning stub, more cash would be added for the next drawing. The crowds were so large on these nights that they filled the lobby and spread out into the street."

Sometimes, special events brought everyone together: working stiffs, pretty ladies, business owners, and the families that lived in the area. These events often cut into business, but no one seemed to mind, since it gave them an opportunity to visit with neighbors. The enthusiasm and excitement of the moment always brought people together. Friendships formed and sometimes led to long-lasting relationships. Occasionally, a pretty lady and a working stiff would connect, run off together, and never be seen on B Street again.

One special event was the second visit of President Franklin D. Roosevelt. He had come to view the progress on the dam. Hundreds of people came to see him. Everyone was thankful that he supported the construction of the dam. It had put thousands to work. Everyone had faith in the president and knew he was doing all he could to help with the problems of the Depression. The town of Grand Coulee had great respect for the president. As one of the working stiffs put it simply, "I didn't know President Roosevelt, but he knew me."

Most businesses on B Street closed for the day in honor of the president's visit. The pretty ladies took time off from their work and went down to the dam site to show their support. Many of the women were excited to have a chance to see the president of the United States up close, in their own backyard.

Seven state patrolmen on motorcycles led a motorcade that carried the president and other dignitaries to the vista house above the construction site. Along the route, President Roosevelt waved at thousands of children and well-wishers, pretty ladies included.

Another special event took place on November 1, 1938, when everyone gathered at the Silver Dollar and other popular hangouts on B Street to listen to the radio. Most of the bars and taverns were overflowing with pretty ladies and construction workers. The excitement mounted as they awaited the start of the horserace of the century. Seabiscuit, the country's new hero, was to race the great thoroughbred War Admiral at Pimlico, in Baltimore. War Admiral was the favorite, but most who were experiencing hard times favored Seabiscuit. The entire country admired this remarkable thoroughbred. They loved his unusual way of running and his ability to come from behind. One of the pretty ladies observed. "Seabiscuit's method of running is actually humorous. When the 'Biscuit runs, his legs thrash about every which way. It reminds me of an eggbeater."

When their favorite ran away from War Admiral to win the race, B Street went wild. Everyone celebrated, throughout the day and night. This was a time of rejoicing when sex was put on the back burner once again, and men and women enjoyed themselves as fans of this great American icon, Seabiscuit. The pretty ladies did not make much money that evening, but the bets they had placed on Seabiscuit made up for the losses.

No one knew for sure how many women plied their trade on B Street. While they lived and worked there, they considered themselves businesswomen, and many conducted themselves very professionally with their clients. Some regularly sent money home to help support their families, while others saved much of their profits for the future. All hoped they would have better lives when the Depression ended. Many would later marry, have children, and enjoy happy family lives.

7

WOO DIP

Julian and his family got little sleep that first night they spent near the Grand Coulee Dam construction site. Dewey was the only one who slept through all the noise from the huge machines that operated nonstop twenty-four hours a day.

Julian and Dewey were up early the next morning, filled with excitement about their new surroundings and all the possibilities that lay before them. They could not believe what they saw as they neared B Street on that spring morning in 1935. As they drove up the hill, leaving Grand Coulee's Midway Avenue behind, they could hear the noise of The Street before they got there. Julian maneuvered the Model T along the dusty street, trying not to hit the throngs of white people crossing from one side to the other. They were amazed at the wooden boardwalks and the number of taverns that lined both sides of the street. Cars were all over the place, parked or stirring up volumes of dust as they passed.

What they witnessed on B Street was much different from the sights and sounds of the quiet little town of Inchelium. It was early morning, but B Street was full of activity, and the noise was constant.

Dewey smiled and nodded. He observed the activity on the street with interest. Both he and Julian were surprised at the large number of good-looking women. They wondered why there were so many.

Since it was early, they decided to go into a small café and order some coffee. They seated themselves in a booth, near a window, and observed the people milling about outside. They studied the men busily working on several buildings, just across from them, that would soon be places of business. The sawing of boards and the hammering of nails reverberated even inside the café.

Outside again, they checked both sides of the street until they came to the Hi Dam Hotel, where a "For Rent" sign had been placed in the window of a small space with an entrance off the boardwalk. Julian studied the interior through the small window. He was pleased to see that there were water pipes installed in the back wall. He wanted to take a closer look.

Dewey peered through the window and thought the space seemed small. He wondered how many people could fit inside and asked Julian if it was big enough.

Julian looked inside again and shrugged. He reminded Dewey that he and Mary did not have much money and that it might be wise to start out small.

The two men went next door and inquired about the owner of the space. They were told that he might be found at the tavern about a block down the street.

Julian and Dewey found the owner sitting in a bar having a beer and talking to the bartender. When he learned that Julian wanted to set up a Chinese restaurant, he became enthusiastic. He loved Chinese food, he said. Every time he went to Spokane, he enjoyed eating at a Chinese restaurant along the Spokane River, where the food was great. There were no Chinese restaurants in town, so there would be no competition.

Julian knew he would have to do some remodeling to make the space work. He could get help from a friend back home who was a good carpenter. The owner was open to any changes Julian needed to make in order to get his new venture started.

As they discussed the rent, Julian did not hide the fact that he was nearly down and out. After he'd been in business for a while, he would be making enough money to pay the required amount. The owner studied Julian. He could sense that Julian was honest and filled with determination about his endeavor. He decided to let them try it for a month or so and wait to see what happened.

The owner drew up a handwritten contract and presented it to Julian to sign. He reached into his pocket, pulled out a set of keys, unhooked one, and gave it to Julian. They shook hands, and the owner wished Julian good luck.

Julian and Dewey drove back across the river to their camp. Mary would be happy to know they had found a place. Julian slapped his thigh and happily exclaimed that it looked like they were in business. Dewey smiled in agreement.

They pulled up to the tent, and Pickles greeted them with his stubby tail wagging. Mary emerged from the tent full of questions.

Julian got out and petted Pickles. Mary was excited to learn they had found a place and had signed a rental agreement. The place was on the first floor of the Hi Dam Hotel, and there was a room upstairs big enough for the family to live in. Julian looked around and asked where the children were. Luana was napping, but Lawney was sitting at the edge of the hill, watching the construction of the dam. Their son had been sitting there for the last hour. He found the construction of the dam and the large number of men at work fascinating.

Julian suggested that they return to Inchelium to see if Jerome

Quill would be willing to help them remodel their new space. Turning it into a restaurant would take work. With Jerome's expert carpentry, they would be able to open sooner. Mary agreed. She knew Jerome was the best carpenter in Inchelium. Early in the afternoon, the family traveled back to their hometown. Dewey stayed behind, with hopes of finding a job.

Julian's timing was good. Jerome had not worked for a while and was anxious to have something to do. He was pleased that Julian needed help. Jerome had never been to Grand Coulee and was curious about the dam. Since he and Julian were friends, he would not charge very much and wouldn't expect any pay until Julian and Mary started making money.

The next day, Jerome rode back to the dam with Julian and the family. Julian, Mary, and the children would move into the room above the restaurant, but Jerome would have to camp out. Jerome shrugged. That was fine with him. He actually preferred it. The air was better outside, he advised Julian. His wife, Florence, preferred living in a house, but he liked it better outside, closer to nature. He slept better.

In the morning, Julian drove Jerome and the family to B Street. Everyone was excited to see where the new restaurant would be. All were curious about The Street.

Julian parked the Model T in front of the Hi Dam Hotel, and everyone got out of the car to take a look at the place. They shaded their eyes as they peered in through the windows.

Julian unlocked the door, and they all went inside. After studying the space with Mary and pacing off the interior, he explained to Jerome what they would like to have built, where the kitchen should be situated, and where the restrooms would be once the plumbing was in place. Jerome followed Julian around, making mental notes on the materials he would need. He did not use working drawings to direct him. Jerome had the ability to visualize a project. Once he did that, he could begin work. He thought he could finish in about a week with some help from Julian.

Jerome wrote down his list of materials and gave it to Julian, who agreed that all the items were necessary and that he could afford to purchase them. He thought that if he presented the rental agreement to the lumberyard and the hardware store, they might allow him to put the costs on a tab to be paid later.

While Jerome worked, Julian and Mary drove down to Grand Coulee to search for used chairs and tables. They looked for pots, pans, dishes, and other kitchen equipment. Julian had seen a second-hand shop on Midway Avenue, and he hoped they could find what they needed there. Afterward, they visited a meat market and grocery stores where they could get supplies once they opened their business. They didn't have much money, and they were going to have to make everything last.

During the next week, Jerome worked efficiently at constructing the walls of the kitchen. Within a few days, he had installed the restroom enclosures. The plumbing would have to wait until the sewer systems were in place. Electricians and then plumbers came in to connect the power and hook up the water lines. Julian and Mary found only a few tables and chairs in downtown Grand Coulee, so they decided to install one more booth. By the end of the week, Jerome had made three booths. The space in the dining area was so small that he could not add more. As Jerome was putting the finishing touches on the kitchen, the supplies and kitchen equipment arrived. Later, Mary and the children came by with the food. Mary was pleased with the progress Jerome had made in setting up the restaurant. She knew he was a good carpenter and made every hour count.

Meanwhile, Dewey had landed a job at the dam working for an excavation contractor. The work was hard and dirty. At the end of his workday, he could not wait to clean up and get something cold to drink. After sitting in the Silver Dollar, enjoying a few beers, he was happy to learn he could be served at the taverns on B Street. Afterward, he walked to the restaurant and watched as Jerome completed his work for the day.

The owner of the hotel and restaurant space came in a number of times to check on their progress. He admired Jerome's work; things looked good. He couldn't wait for a good dish of Chinese food. He really liked pork fried rice with fresh bean sprouts. It was the bean sprouts that made fried rice so good, he explained. Chow mein was another of his favorites. He hoped the food would be as good as the food at the restaurant in Spokane. Julian promised it would be better.

The owner studied the kitchen area and saw that they needed a stove. He told Julian not to worry. He knew of a family who owned two. One was sitting in their backyard under some canvas, getting old and rusty, but it was still in good condition. Julian realized he might get a good deal. A few days later, with Jerome's and Dewey's help, Julian moved the old wood-burning cookstove into the newly finished kitchen. He proudly showed it to his family.

While the grown-ups worked, the children played with Pickles on the boardwalk in front of the hotel. When they tired of that, they walked up and down B Street with Dewey, looking into the windows of the different stores that were being built. They found that B Street was a very busy place. The four shared the boardwalks with hundreds of workingmen as they, too, walked the streets. Many would stop in at taverns and return to the boardwalks in good spirits. The children found the workingmen very friendly. Even Pickles liked them. He wagged his stubby tail when they talked to him or bent down to pet him.

After a week and a half, the restaurant was finished. Both the dining and kitchen areas seemed smaller now that everything was in place. The walls and ceiling were a warm off-white color. Everything looked brand-new. Julian, Mary, and Jerome stood back to admire their work. Jerome studied his workmanship. Carpentry was important to him. He inspected the details of the booths he had constructed and smiled with satisfaction.

Mary was concerned that the space was too small, but she finally shrugged and said that it would have to do. Julian agreed. It was too late to change course now. They would wait to see if it was big enough for them to make any money. He could see now that it was going to be a lot of hard work. They would have to cook, wait tables, wash dishes, and cashier. Someone would also have to buy supplies and keep the kitchen stocked. It would not be easy for two people. Julian wondered if they would be able to handle it.

Julian's greatest concern was the food. He was not a good cook. Actually, he didn't like to cook. He didn't like the idea of spending his time inside a kitchen, bending over a hot stove, and much preferred the outdoors, where the air was cool and fresh. He had eaten in a Chinese restaurant only three or four times and really didn't know that much about the food. He knew a little about Filipino food, but the only similarity between Chinese and Filipino food was rice. He knew how to cook rice, and that was about it.

Jerome sat quietly as Julian and Mary talked. He removed cigarette paper from its folder, carefully rolled a smoke, and lit it. Jerome asked what they were going to call the place now that it was ready to open. Julian shrugged. He hadn't thought about it.

Mary lit a cigarette and inhaled. She let the smoke out slowly. She had been thinking about this for some time. Since they were going to have a Chinese restaurant, it should have a Chinese name. She asked them what they thought about the name Woo Dip?

"Woo Dip? Is that a Chinese name?" Julian asked. It sounded kind of funny to him. What did it mean? Where had she heard it?

Mary didn't know if the name was Chinese or not. She didn't know what it meant. It sounded Chinese to her, and she certainly liked it.

Julian shrugged again and agreed. The name of their new restaurant would be Woo Dip. They would have to make a sign and hang it outside so that people would know about it. Mary nodded and looked at Jerome. That wouldn't be a problem, Jerome thought. He could start right away and have it finished in the morning. Within the hour, he had covered a large board with fresh white paint. When it dried, he would paint the name of the restaurant on it.

Early the next day, Jerome painted the words "Woo Dip" in big red letters on one side of the sign. He found some wire and screws in his toolbox and went outside. Julian followed, carrying a ladder. When the sign was up, Julian and Mary were ready for business. The three stood back on the boardwalk to admire the sign. Mary was pleased. This would be her first place of business, a business that had been planned and realized through her efforts as well as Julian's. It would be her dream come true.

That afternoon, Julian and Mary opened the Woo Dip restaurant. Three adjoining businesses and the owner of the hotel sent bouquets of flowers to celebrate the event. The children loved the excitement of opening day. They loved the new restaurant and enjoyed the fragrance of the flowers. Mary told them that they should stay outside and play, or go upstairs to their room above the restaurant. Pickles would have to remain outside because the law would not permit dogs inside a place of eating. Lawney defended Pickles. He wasn't a dog, he argued. Pickles was a member of the family, like everyone else. Mary was firm, so the children went upstairs to their room with Pickles close behind.

On the first day of business, three attractive women came in and seated themselves in one of the booths. They ordered from the handwritten menu Mary had prepared the night before. Mary suspected that they were ladies of the evening, but she was not sure. A short time later, the owner of the hotel arrived and seated himself in the booth next to the women. He ordered his favorite Chinese dish, pork fried rice. Afterward, a few workingmen sat down in another booth.

The clanging of pots and pans echoed in the kitchen, as Julian did his best to prepare pork fried rice and chop suey. Before the day ended, he had learned to make a passable egg foo yung. It didn't really look like egg foo yung, but the taste was somewhat close. Although pork noodles seemed like an easy dish to prepare, Julian had difficulty with it. He knew he would have to work on the dish before anyone would accept it and not send it back to the kitchen.

When Julian was not preparing an order, he washed pots, pans, dishes, and silverware. The noise he made in the kitchen was sometimes distracting, and Mary had to stick her head through the door and tell him to quiet down so he wouldn't disturb the customers. Mary served as the waitress and cashier. She brought empty dishes to the kitchen and cleaned and set tables for new customers.

After closing their doors on the first day of business, Julian and Mary were exhausted. They sat in silence in the dining room, too tired to speak.

Dewey, who had come in earlier to visit, sat with them. Mary poured everyone a cup of coffee and sat down in a booth with her legs stretched out. Julian went into the kitchen and brought out a bottle of Cobbs Creek whiskey. He took a long drink from the bottle and handed it to Dewey, who poured some into his coffee. Mary rolled a smoke and handed the small sack of tobacco and packet of cigarette paper to Dewey. She yawned and sighed deeply. She had never felt so drained of energy in her entire life. Running a restaurant was not easy. It was the hardest work she had ever done. As soon as they could afford it, they would need to hire help.

Julian stood, chewing his snoose, and went into the kitchen to spit in the garbage can. When he returned, he expressed his concern. He was going to have to find a Chinese cookbook. He wished he had thought of that sooner. The chop suey he had made today hadn't looked right. He had tasted it, and something was missing. It wasn't like the dish they had eaten in Spokane.

Mary had noticed that the three women who were seated next to the door didn't touch most of their food. The owner hadn't seemed too pleased with his fried rice, either. She suggested that Julian should maybe find that cookbook soon, or they wouldn't have any repeat customers. Julian went back into the kitchen to spit again.

During the following days, more customers came. Most were workingmen. Almost all were young, and all were hungry. The menu Mary had prepared was not large, and Julian was thankful for that. He was having difficulty preparing the dishes that customers were ordering. In spite of his efforts, no two dishes looked alike, nor did they taste alike. He was thankful for the ignorance of the young workingmen. Most of them had come from small towns where there were no Chinese restaurants, and none really knew what authentic Chinese food tasted like.

The women customers, to Julian's dismay, proved to be more of a challenge. Many had come from Seattle, where they had eaten at restaurants in Chinatown. They knew what good Chinese food was supposed to taste like. More than once, the women returned their orders to the kitchen, and he was forced to try again.

After the Woo Dip opened, Jerome remained at B Street for nearly a week. But the constant noise and activity began to tire him. He wanted to return to Inchelium. He was weary of the thousands of people. It seemed that the workingmen were always drunk and fighting over women. He could not see the wisdom of fighting over women, especially women who did not even belong to them. He began to wonder about the priorities of white men.

Jerome also missed the peace and quiet of Inchelium, the trees and mountains, and Twin Lakes. He missed the elders, like Cashmere and the others who spent their time basking in the sunlight in front of the General Store, and he missed Florence's home cooking. He was beginning to tire of Julian's unsuccessful attempts to cook good-tasting food. Most of all, he missed Indians. Mike, his youngest son, arrived to drive him back to Inchelium a few days later.

After the Woo Dip opened, the moccasin telegraph once again went to work in Inchelium. Many residents wanted to go to Grand Coulee. They wanted to see B Street with their own eyes. They had heard that Julian and Mary had a successful restaurant and that the food was good. They were surprised when they found out it was a Chinese restaurant. No one in Inchelium had eaten Chinese food, and they were curious about it. They wondered where and how Julian and Mary had learned to cook it.

When they could afford it, many journeyed to Grand Coulee to visit B Street and the Woo Dip restaurant. Visitors from Inchelium were surprised at the number of white people on B Street. They could not believe the noise that came from the loudspeakers outside the many taverns. The young Indian men were impressed with the attractive women who walked the street and sat in the taverns and restaurants. The women appeared well dressed and quite charming. The men were surprised and amused by the fights over women that started in the taverns and often ended up on the boardwalks.

It was impossible to compare Inchelium and B Street. Visitors from Inchelium were astounded by the number of cars driving by on the streets and parked at the curbs. Several noticed that there were no horses. The streets were relatively clean, and passersby did not have to pick their way around piles of horse manure, unlike on Main Street in Inchelium. The Indians wondered where all the horses were corralled on this heavily populated street.

Many times, Mary's friends and other younger women from Inchelium and Nespelem who wanted work or excitement journeyed to Grand Coulee. They would ask Mary to teach them how to wait tables and cashier at the Woo Dip. Mary patiently taught them and put them to work. Some would stay for a few weeks, and others for a few months. All were grateful to Mary for taking the time to teach them and giving them the opportunity to be employed. They enjoyed the independence of being away from home, and many grew to like the excitement on B Street. At the same time, Mary appreciated their help in the restaurant because it gave her more time to be with her children.

Many of the women from Inchelium and Nespelem found that the workingmen welcomed their presence on B Street and would buy them drinks. Most nights, the women spent hours dancing. Occasionally, a workingman rented a room and invited a woman to spend the night with him. Eventually, most of the women returned to Inchelium, but others moved on to bigger cities like Spokane or Seattle and experienced other adventures.

Every day, the children took a walk with their dog Pickles, down one side of B Street and then up the other. By this time, their parents felt confident that they would be safe. They trusted the friendships the children had made with the men and women on B Street. Since Lawney and Luana were the only children on The Street, everyone made a point of looking after them. Often, they were greeted on their walks by the workingmen who frequented the restaurant. When they reached the Silver Dollar, the children always stopped to talk to the women gathered outside and received gifts of chewing gum. Then the brother and sister turned around and went back to the family's restaurant. This pleasant ritual became a part of the children's daily walks up and down B Street.

In her free time, and when the children were napping, Mary would record the day's events in her diary. It became a ritual for her. She never missed a day. As time went on, she found there was a lot to write about. Life on B Street was exciting. It differed greatly from the quiet life she had known in Inchelium. The whites were loud and energetic and expended much energy on whatever they did. In contrast, the people back home on the reservation were quiet, disciplined, and thoughtful.

Mary's diary recorded in detail everything the family experienced each day: initial reactions of visitors from Inchelium; customers' responses to the food Julian cooked; the adventures of Lawney, Luana, and Pickles as they walked B Street; the frivolity of the pretty ladies who frequented the restaurant; hard times and long hours spent running the business; and the reprieve they enjoyed by going to movies in their free time.

One night, at the end of July in 1935, the Hi Dam Hotel caught fire. Those who were responsible for fighting fires had only primitive means at their disposal. Before they could contain the fire, it had destroyed part of the kitchen at the Woo Dip, and Julian and Mary had to close the restaurant for repairs.

After studying the situation, Julian decided that remaining at the hotel was not a good idea. He suggested they search for a bigger space that would give them room to serve more customers. Mary agreed.

The owner of the hotel was aware that the place he had rented to them was too small. He wished them luck in finding another. A few days later, Julian and Mary found a vacant building a few blocks up the street. They studied the building and agreed it was more suitable for their needs. The next day, they met the owner, who explained that they would have to sign a three-year lease. Julian and Mary had no experience in such matters. Three years seemed like a long time. They decided to get advice from someone knowledgeable before they signed.

Mary remembered seeing a sign that read "Joe Wicks, Attorney" on Fourth Street. That afternoon, she walked with Lawney down to Joe Wicks's office, located near Midway Avenue. She saw a tall man, who appeared to be about her age, sitting behind a desk. He clearly looked Indian. Behind him, an impressive wall-to-wall bookcase held dozens of books on the practice of law and a photo of his family. He stood and extended his hand to welcome her. She explained her concern about signing a three-year lease and said that she needed help in understanding the lease agreement. Her husband had no experience in such matters, either. Mr. Wicks agreed to look at the building and study the lease agreement. Before Mary and her son left, she learned that the tall man was part Cherokee. He was originally from Oklahoma. The two shook hands again as they parted.

The next day, Mr. Wicks walked up to B Street. He came to the hotel room where Julian and the family lived. He had looked at the new building and judged that it was in good shape. He thought the rental price was fair and suggested that they take out fire insurance since there had been a number of fires in the area. Julian and Mary were pleased with the advice provided by Mr. Wicks and decided to rent the building.

Later, Mary learned that Mr. Wicks had been a member of Eliot Ness's "Untouchables" during the Prohibition years and was instrumental in placing the mobster Al Capone behind bars for tax evasion. He was also associated with the Treasury Department and with the FBI as a special agent. Before that, he had studied law at George Washington University in Washington, D.C. He served in France during World War I and in 1921 became a deputy U.S. Marshal in Oklahoma.

Julian and Mary were impressed. They felt it was admirable that a person who was part Indian could accomplish that much in spite of the prejudice directed against Indians at the time. They were also surprised to learn that Mr. Wicks, a Republican, was the first city attorney in Grand Coulee, a town totally populated by Democrats. Years later, in 1946, Mr. Wicks would be appointed a superior court judge in Okanogan County. He was to serve in that position for fifteen years and would be admired and respected by many during his time on the bench.

Jerome came back to Grand Coulee to work on the renovation of the building. In three weeks, the restaurant was ready. The children

Joe Wicks with wife Mabel and daughters Mary and Baby JoAnn, Grand Coulee, 1936. Courtesy Mary Wicks Brucker.

Joe Wicks at home in Omak, 1939. Courtesy Mary Wicks Brucker.

were happy with the new location. The dining room was bigger, which gave them more room to play when the restaurant was closed. A good-size sandlot in the back offered privacy and a place to play for the children and their dog. They could have as much fun as they wanted without being closely watched by their mother.

Behind the restaurant, Jerome built a floor and sidewalls four feet in height. He stretched canvas overhead and secured it to the sidewalls in place of a roof. This enclosure became the new home of the family of four. Kerosene and gas lamps provided light inside. During the cold months, a small oil heater from Rawe's Hardware Store kept the family warm.

Everyone, including Pickles, was pleased with the family's new quarters. Julian and Mary were relieved that they would no longer have to pay rent for the small room at the Hi Dam Hotel. Lawney and Luana had always enjoyed living in a tent. They had lived out of doors many times. The children remembered last winter, when they had lived in a tent at Twin Lakes. Before that, they had camped each summer at Kettle Falls when the great chinook salmon came upriver in June. They always felt closer to nature when they were out of doors. But most of all, the children were happy that they had their own private sandlot just outside the tent.

8

SHOW BUSINESS

Julian loved music and practiced on his Dobro guitar as often as he could, whenever he was not working at the Woo Dip restaurant. After he had left the Philippines and was living in Honolulu, he learned to play a variety of stringed instruments. Later, he became a professional musician while he was living in Seattle's Chinatown. He joined an all-Filipino orchestra of thirty musicians who played only stringed instruments. They were always in demand at certain clubs in the Seattle area. Some would travel in smaller groups to Alaska and perform for other Filipinos who worked in the fish canneries.

Julian remembered fondly those good but hard days before he was married. He remembered when he had traveled east of the mountains to Spokane and farther east to Wallace, Idaho, where he worked as a salesman for the Turner Music Store, selling guitars and ukuleles. The store's owner was the father of Lana Turner, the famous movie star.

As Julian practiced, he thought of his two children, Lawney and Luana. He was pleased that they had adjusted to their new home on B Street and were always eager to test new ground with no complaint. He trusted his children's ability to navigate B Street. He knew that he could depend on their friendships with many of the women and workingmen. Julian was comfortable with these thoughts, knowing that his children were safe. It made life much easier for him and Mary as they worked to build a business to support the family. The children were well behaved. They were never a problem. He was pleased and very proud of them.

One day, Julian decided it was time to teach his four-year-old how to play a stringed instrument. Julian loved Hawaiian music, which he had learned to play in Honolulu, and he felt he must pass this knowledge on to his son. The ukulele would be first, and after that, he would concentrate on the guitar. He had purchased two Dobro guitars and a ukulele, and he treasured all three. Years earlier, before the children were born, Julian had taught Mary how to chord, and she had sometimes accompanied him on the second guitar as he played the steel. He thought that, with instruction, his son could do this, too.

The next day, Julian began lessons. He taught Lawney the elementary fingering positions on the ukulele. Within a few weeks, Lawney could accompany his father on simple Hawaiian songs. Julian was pleased to see his son learning so quickly. Lawney had inherited his father's feel for timing and ear for melody. Julian sensed that his son had inherited some of his ability to understand and appreciate music. It wouldn't be long before Lawney would be able to play on his own.

While shopping for groceries one day, Mary noticed a small Hawaiian grass skirt for sale in a pawnshop. She thought that the skirt would fit two-year-old Luana if it was trimmed and the waistline was altered. Mary knew her daughter was very bright and had understanding beyond her years.

Mary bought the grass skirt and made the necessary adjustments so that Luana could wear it. Luana was delighted with the unusual skirt. She did not know what it was for, but it felt good. The skirt made swishing sounds as she twirled.

Mary was devising a plan. She retrieved two Hawaiian leis that had been packed away and shortened them to fit the children. She put the leis around their necks and stepped back to admire them. She was satisfied with their outfits. With more practice, they would be ready to perform.

Mary decided that if Luana could learn to dance, Lawney could accompany her on the ukulele. People would enjoy watching the children perform as she and Julian once had, when they appeared in the towns of Kettle Falls, Marcus, Meyers Falls, and Colville. She smiled as she remembered her stage name, Aloha, and recalled dancing the hula Julian had taught her as he played the steel guitar. The audiences in those small towns had appreciated the Hawaiian music, and the two had enjoyed performing for them. She remembered that those were carefree and happy times, before the children were born.

Early each morning, before the restaurant opened, Julian and Mary spent time teaching their children to perform as they once had. Within weeks, Lawney and Luana were becoming very good. Sometimes, Dewey Hall came in and poured a glass of Cobbs Creek, lit a cigarette, and sat back to enjoy the children's performance as they practiced. Dewey beamed as he told Julian that he thought the children were ready for the "big time."

Julian and Mary were sitting quietly in the dining room early one morning after a hard night's work. Mary was sipping coffee, and Julian had poured himself a glass of Cobbs Creek. He announced that he thought the children were ready to perform. They had really improved over the past few weeks. He had never thought Lawney would play so well, so early. His son was a natural on the uke. Mary agreed that the children were ready. She was especially proud of her young daughter's ability to dance the hula. The child was able to perform steps that usually gave adults trouble. Mary believed, too, that the children were ready to perform in front of an audience. She knew they would be a hit.

Julian began to make plans. He talked to the manager of one of the dance halls and asked if Lawney and Luana could perform there. The manager thought it was a good idea. The kids could perform three numbers. He was in business to make money, but he thought he could spare that much time. Julian accepted.

The next day, a crowd of working stiffs, taxi dancers, and pretty ladies moved off the dance floor so that the children could perform their numbers. Julian sang "Little Grass Shack," a popular Hawaiian song he had learned in Honolulu. Lawney diligently strummed the chords on his ukulele. Luana danced and performed some intricate hula steps, enjoying the swish of her skirt. "Aloha Oe" was the next number, and Lawney chorded as Julian played the lead. The last song was "Sweet Leilani." They got a round of applause after each number. The crowd was delighted with the young performers. The pretty ladies were especially pleased. Many of them knew Lawney and Luana and tossed coins onto the floor in appreciation.

Everyone in the dance hall had a good time that afternoon. The children bowed when their performance ended, and people in the audience began throwing more coins to show their appreciation. Lawney was surprised and delighted to realize that the money was for them. He encouraged Luana to pick up the coins quickly, so they could run back home and count them.

During the children's performance, a spectator from Spokane was taken by what he saw. He introduced himself to Julian as Jim

Lawney and Luana Reyes, performing at B Street, 1935. Courtesy Mary "Aloha" Reyes.

Chamberlain. He thought he could arrange to have the children perform in a number of small towns between Spokane and Grand Coulee Dam. Julian told Mary about the idea, and they both agreed it would be a lot of fun and a good break from the tedious work of running a restaurant. It would be a well-earned vacation for all of them.

A month later, Julian got a letter from Mr. Chamberlain. He had arranged for Julian and his family to perform in mid-August at movie theaters in Sprague, Ritzville, Odessa, Wilson Creek, and Soap Lake. In those days, it was not uncommon for vaudeville acts to appear onstage during the intermission between movies. The family could expect payment for their entertainment and could also keep any tips they might receive from the audience. The people in these small eastern Washington towns had never seen live Hawaiian entertainment, and Mr. Chamberlain believed they would enjoy the experience as much as he had.

Julian arranged for help in keeping the restaurant open part-time. He knew that his steady customers would accept the situation since it would last for only a few days.

In each town, the children performed to packed houses. They took the stage during the intermission between the movies of a double feature. Julian situated himself behind a curtain so as not to distract from his children's performance. He played his steel guitar as Lawney chorded to the melody on his ukulele. Julian soon learned that his son was really not that interested in playing a musical instrument. He was more interested in picking up the coins after each performance. Luana was delighted with the attention from the audience. She enjoyed moving and rotating her tiny body to make the grass skirt whirl. She liked the swishing noise the skirt made as she twirled around. Most of all, she loved the applause she and her brother received.

The family spent the days traveling from one small town to the next. After each performance, Julian pitched a tent near the outskirts of the town. He made sure to set up camp close to a creek, which would provide drinking water and a place to bathe and cool off. The children played in the creek with Pickles, who enjoyed it as much as they did. After shopping at the local grocery store, they sat and ate on the bank of the creek. When night fell, Luana, Lawney, and Pickles settled down in the back of the Model T, while Julian and Mary retired to the tent. As they lay quietly preparing to sleep, they could listen to the creek trickling by. The sounds reminded them of other creeks that had flowed past their camps on the reservation. The next day, they traveled to another destination and another performance.

Pickles enjoyed the chance to get away from B Street, and he guarded the Model T when the children were onstage. At every performance, the audience tossed coins onto the stage in appreciation

for the children's efforts. People enjoyed watching the children bow to the applause and then scramble about picking up the coins. They had never seen such young entertainers perform music that could otherwise be heard only on the radio. Their appreciation increased even more when they learned that Lawney was only four years old and Luana was two.

After their performances, the children counted their money and put it in one of Lawney's old socks, and Lawney hid it under the blankets in the back of the Model T. By the time they reached home, the sock was half full of pennies, nickels, and dimes. The children were happy with their accomplishments. They enjoyed seeing new places and being the center of attention of so many adults. It was the first time they had earned money and saved it.

Julian was pleased with the way his children had performed on tour. The audiences had loved them. He continued instructing Lawney. With practice, his son could tune the ukulele by ear. Julian was very proud. In his spare time, he began instructing students who were interested in learning to play the steel guitar and the ukulele. As time went on, he realized he was much more skilled at teaching music on his beloved Dobros than at slaving over a hot stove trying to cook Chinese food.

Back on B Street, the family enjoyed more attention than ever. The children were pleased with the money they had earned on tour and delighted when Mary gave them permission to buy candy at Atwater's Drug Store. She allowed them to buy one candy bar each, once a week, and made them promise to brush their teeth after eat-

(Opposite, top) *Dewey, Mary, Julian, and student near B Street, 1936. Courtesy Julian S. Reyes.*

(Opposite, bottom) *Student, Mary, and Julian practicing steel guitars and ukulele at B Street, 1936. Courtesy Mary "Aloha" Reyes.*

ing the candy. The children enjoyed their newfound wealth and the opportunity to spend it on things they liked. Lawney bought his favorite candy bar, a Butterfinger, and, with her brother's help, Luana happily bought her favorite, a Baby Ruth. Afterward, they went out to the tent behind the restaurant, retrieved Lawney's old sock from under the mattress, and counted the money they had left for another day.

9

THE CHINA MAN

The Greyhound bus arrived at the small station in Grand Coulee in the early afternoon. It had made its daily trip from Spokane and was en route to Nespelem and then to the Okanogan Valley farther west. Harry Wong stepped from the bus carrying a well-worn suitcase and a decrepit violin case. He was a short man, barely five feet, two inches, and of medium build. Harry was in his mid-twenties. He had a friendly face, and his eyes twinkled.

Harry looked around at the unfamiliar surroundings. Midway Avenue was busy with people walking to their different destinations. Automobiles stirred pockets of dust as they passed. Harry was a stranger to these parts, and he found the small town intriguing, so unlike Spokane.

It was mid-September 1935, and Harry had come to Grand Coulee hoping to find a job. It really didn't matter what kind of job, but he was hoping to find employment as a cook. That was his specialty. He had worked for three years as a houseboy for a rich white family in Spokane. After that, he had been employed at a Chinese restaurant for nearly six years. Harry started as a dishwasher and handyman. Later, he became a waiter and then learned to cook.

But now, he had tired of the large city and wanted to start over in another place. He wanted to live in a small town and experience life in a quiet community with fewer people. Harry hoped one day to own his own business. He wanted to be in charge and have others working for him. This had been his dream since he was sixteen and left Canton, China, to come to America.

He remembered that life in Canton was hard. Many of the people there were barely making it. It was very difficult to find jobs. That was the reason many young Chinese left their beloved homeland to seek their fortunes in America.

The Chinese who journeyed to the States did not know that they would experience extreme prejudice once they arrived. They found it difficult to learn American ways. The English language did not come easy. Most did not adapt easily to their new lives and kept to themselves. Many had a hard time adjusting to the food Americans ate. They soon found ways of obtaining Chinese foods, spices, and vegetables in the larger cities along the coast and managed to prepare the dishes they had eaten when they lived in China. This made it easier for them to live in a foreign land so far away.

The Chinese found it hard to make friends with white people who regarded them as inferior and found security among themselves when confronted with discrimination. In the large cities of Portland, San Francisco, and Seattle, they lived together quietly, keeping their resentment to themselves, and developed communities and societies that were totally Chinese. They never shared their innermost thoughts with white people. They had learned, over the years, never to confide in or trust them.

At the bus station, Harry learned that a Chinese restaurant was open for business up on B Street. The man who operated the station told him how to get there. Harry picked up his suitcase and his beloved violin case and walked up the steep hill to B Street. He could hear the activity before he got there. The blare of the loudspeakers from the many taverns nearly deafened him. Hundreds of workingmen were milling about. A clutter of small businesses lined both sides of the street. Harry was surprised by the many attractive women he saw. He wondered why they were there and why they were dressed so scantily. All the women wore silk stockings with the seam running down the back of the leg and fashionable high-heeled shoes.

There were a number of buildings under construction. The hammering of nails and the sawing of boards added to the noise. As he tried to make his way through hundreds of young workingmen and dozens of pretty young women, he wondered if he had made a mistake in coming to such a place.

Following the directions he had been given, Harry found the Chinese restaurant. It was small and nondescript compared to the restaurants where he had worked in Spokane. He opened the door and walked inside, leaving behind the mass of people and noise outside. About a half dozen customers were seated at tables and booths. He found an empty booth, placed his suitcase and violin case on the floor, and sat down.

The waitress set a glass of cold water and a menu in front of him and waited to take his order. Harry was not hungry but decided to order a plate of bok choy with Chinese mushrooms and prawns. The waitress explained that the dish was not on the menu, so Harry settled for a bowl of chow mein. He received his order and attempted to eat but found the food offensive to his taste and pushed it aside. He asked for a pot of tea. The waitress politely informed him that there was no tea, just coffee. Harry was surprised—a Chinese restaurant with no tea. He was not really fond of coffee but decided not to make an issue of it and ordered a cup anyway.

The waitress brought the coffee. She studied Harry and surmised that he might be from somewhere in the Orient. She wondered what brought him to these parts. She had never seen an Asian person in any of the small towns of eastern Washington.

She asked if she could sit across from him as he sipped his coffee. They talked. The waitress had difficulty understanding Harry. Many of the words he spoke were unclear to her. She saw that English did not come easy for him. She learned that he had traveled that day from Spokane in search of work. She sat in disbelief when she found out that he was a Chinese cook, skilled in the traditional foods of his country.

Harry sensed that the waitress was having a difficult time believing him. He got up and walked to the kitchen, signaling her to follow.

Harry entered the kitchen and frowned as he saw the cook laboring over an old wood-burning stove. He knew the only way to prepare Chinese dishes was on a gas stove. His eyes searched carefully for a wok, but he did not see one. He shook his head in disappointment and reached for a large frying pan partly filled with cooked rice.

Once again, he looked around the kitchen in search of barbecued pork. Not finding any, he settled for some roast pork. Next, he took two eggs out of the icebox and grabbed an onion from a sack on the floor. Harry quickly cut the meat into small pieces and sliced the onion faster than the eyes of the waitress could follow. He looked around the kitchen and frowned once again, this time looking for bean sprouts and soy sauce. The cook enthusiastically handed him a small bottle of soy sauce, but there were no bean sprouts to be found.

Harry was obviously disappointed with what he had to work with but decided to make the best of it. Within minutes, he had finished cooking and dished the contents of the frying pan into two bowls. He placed the bowls in front of the cook and the waitress and smiled, directing them to eat.

When they were finished, the waitress smiled. She found the food very tasty. The cook agreed. It was the best pork fried rice he had ever eaten.

The cook and waitress introduced themselves to Harry as Julian and Mary. Julian eagerly removed his apron and handed it to Harry, asking him when he could begin work.

The three left the kitchen, and Harry seated himself in the booth once again. He asked for paper and a pencil, and Mary brought him a tablet and a pencil from the kitchen.

Harry proceeded to make a list of the things he needed. The best place to get supplies was Chinatown in Seattle. He knew where to get the best buys. When he had finished the list, he handed it to Julian. It was written in Chinese. Mary looked at Harry's list but could not decipher it and gave it back to Julian.

That afternoon, Mary introduced Harry to Lawney and Luana. They sensed the joy their parents were feeling about their new Chinese chef. As Harry extended his hand to them, the children somehow felt that he would become an important part of their lives, an important part of their family.

Julian took Harry to Jim O'Brien's cabins, located close by. He told Harry the cabins were inexpensive and clean. Jim was a good man and very considerate. Harry was pleased and agreed that the room he saw would be adequate for his needs.

Within a week and a half, Harry received the supplies he had ordered from Seattle. He carried the boxes into the kitchen, carefully unpacked them, and positioned the items near the wood-burning stove. He unpacked two woks, one large and one smaller. Harry held up the large wok and smiled as he showed it to Julian. From another box, he took out three knives of different sizes and a large Chinese cleaver. Harry unpacked other strange-looking utensils specifically made for Chinese cooking. Another box held assorted bottles: fish sauce, oyster sauce, ginger, and a variety of jars with Chinese writing on them.

As Julian helped Harry unpack the boxes, he tried to determine the contents of the numerous bottles of sauces. He was awed by what he saw and threw up his arms in dismay. It was no wonder he couldn't cook good Chinese dishes. No one had ever bothered to tell him about all the sauces and spices used in the preparation of authentic Chinese food. Mary just smiled.

Harry grinned as he discovered the box filled with the tea he had ordered. He wondered how Julian and Mary could have thought that they could run a Chinese restaurant without serving tea.

The next week, Harry received three more boxes filled with bowls, dishes, teacups, and teapots, all with Chinese symbols on them. One box contained chopsticks made of bamboo. The biggest box held two large aluminum cooking pots.

Harry was pleased with the deliveries. He smiled broadly when he found a small richly decorated box with more Chinese symbols on it. He handed the box to Lawney and Luana. It was for them.

The children opened it together and found a variety of Chinese candy and fruits inside. The box came from China, and the contents were not available in the United States. Luana and Lawney marveled at the flavors. They had never tasted anything like this. Luana was especially fond of a candy that tasted of ginger. Harry smiled. Lawney's favorite Chinese treat was lychee. He loved the mellow flavor of the fruit inside the fragile brown shells.

The last box contained a Chinese dress made of silk for Mary. An embroidered dragon decorated the upper right shoulder of the beautiful red dress. Harry had bought it for Mary to wear when she waited tables in the restaurant. She was delighted.

Business improved noticeably after Harry started cooking. Julian was happy and relieved to get away from the stove. He did not mind becoming the dishwasher, handyman, and janitor. He felt more at home doing this kind of work. Julian loved being out of doors. He did not fancy himself as a man who spent hours in front of a hot stove cooking for people who did not appreciate his efforts in the first place.

Before Harry took over the cooking, Julian had always found it difficult to chew his snoose and perform his duties at the same time. He usually spit into the garbage can in the kitchen. Sometimes, when he was in a hurry, he missed the can, and Mary would tell him to clean it up. Julian knew that chewing snoose was a nasty habit. He was aware that Mary considered it uncouth. He wished he had never learned it from that Swede up in Alaska when, as a young man, he had worked in the fish canneries. But it was too late now. It had become a habit that he didn't want to break.

As far as Julian was concerned, those days of trying to cook were over. Harry did his best to instruct Julian in the art of cooking fine Chinese food, but Julian proved to be a poor learner. He really was not interested in Chinese cooking. For that matter, he was not interested in any type of cooking. He would cook only when Harry needed some time off, and then only simple dishes.

As weeks turned into months, business steadily got better. Julian

Harry, Julian, and Mary in the Woo Dip kitchen on B Street, 1935.
Courtesy Julian S. Reyes.

and Mary had to hire a second waitress. They were able to keep their prices down because of Harry's ability to shop carefully and plan menus. The customers loved Harry's food and soon became regulars.

Lawney and Luana grew to appreciate Harry's cooking. They enjoyed visiting him in the kitchen and watching him prepare wonderful Chinese dishes with ease. They loved the aroma and unique flavors of his cooking. Lawney especially enjoyed a thin patty of ground beef heavily sprinkled with pepper. The meat was uncooked but very tasty. When Harry was not busy, he prepared it for his gracious customer. Years later, Lawney learned that the tasty dish Harry prepared was the French delicacy steak tartare.

One day, Harry asked Lawney if he knew how to eat with chopsticks. Lawney shook his head. Harry smiled. He gave Lawney a pair of chopsticks and positioned them in the boy's hands. Harry took a pair for himself and proceeded to pick up small pieces of meat from a bowl. Lawney watched intently and started to copy Harry's movements. Within minutes, he was able to grasp the meat and put it down. After that, he ate every meal with the chopsticks Harry had given to him, regardless of whether it was an American or a Chinese dish.

During Harry's free time, he told the children stories about China. When he was in the mood, which was often, he would carefully remove his violin from its case and play simple tunes as the children sat at his feet. Harry could not read music, but he remembered simple songs with easy melodies. Sometimes, he played Chinese songs. This music was different, but the children loved it. Harry was pleased that they liked his music. As he played, he always kept time by tapping his right foot on the floor. He had a big smile on his face and a friendly sparkle in his narrow eyes. Pickles would close his protruding round eyes and howl when Harry hit certain high notes.

The restaurant opened at 2:00 P.M. and served customers until well after midnight. It made for a long working shift. Julian and Mary did not have the energy to open sooner, and they knew their schedule captured the best trade.

Early each morning, after the restaurant closed, Harry began preparing dishes that he would complete the next day. Then he emerged from the kitchen, carrying a pot of tea and a teacup, and joined Julian and Mary. He lit a cigarette and offered the pack to Mary, who took one for herself. Julian stuffed tobacco into his pipe, tamped it, and struck a match to light it. He leaned back and studied the smoke as it hovered, then drifted away. They did this to unwind after a hard night's work.

As Harry sipped his tea, he studied the menu Mary had prepared. The name Woo Dip puzzled him. He asked what it meant. Mary said that she believed it to be Chinese, but he had never heard the words before. The words might be from a Chinese dialect not spoken in Canton, but he was not sure.

Mary folded her arms stubbornly, with a cigarette crimped firmly between her lips, and reiterated her belief that "Woo Dip" must be Chinese. To her, it certainly sounded Chinese. Somewhat in doubt, she would mumble the words "Woo Dip" to herself as she removed the money from the till and began counting the day's receipts.

One morning, after closing, Harry sat at his favorite table with his pot of tea and a small cup. He stretched his legs and leaned back in the chair. It had been a long day, and he was tired. Julian and Mary joined him, and Harry told them of his experiences in Seattle and eastern Washington.

He was only sixteen years old when he left his beloved Canton and made the trip to America. He had been in the Northwest for more than ten years now and had lived in both Seattle and Spokane, where he worked at a variety of jobs. He always managed to support himself, but it had not been easy for him. His last job had been at a Chinese restaurant in Spokane, where he had worked his way up from dishwasher to one of the restaurant's most dependable chefs.

Sometimes, Harry also talked about his early experiences in Canton. It had been very hard to make a living there, and he and many other Chinese came to America to find work. Everybody in Canton was hungry and many were close to starving to death. Mary and Julian could empathize with his experience of poverty. They understood the pain of hunger.

Time passed quickly, and soon Harry began to make a name for himself as a top chef on B Street. The working stiffs and pretty ladies were passing the word. More of them came to eat at the Woo Dip. They liked the food and the prices. Word on The Street was that the Woo Dip had the best food and the lowest prices in town.

Harry made many friends during his time at B Street. A few hours before opening, at 2:00 in the afternoon, he would take his daily exercise by walking down and then up B Street. At first, the small Chinese man walking with deliberate shortened steps, his fingers gently locked behind him, was a novel sight for everyone.

Harry liked peering into storefronts and studying the merchandise on display. Sometimes, he had to dodge men fighting and rolling about on the boardwalks. To many, he seemed foreign and out of place on The Street. But he was always interesting. As time went on, Harry became a center of attention. Everyone grew to appreciate the small unassuming man with the narrow eyes and smiling face. His appearance always seemed to brighten everyone's day.

The next year passed quickly for Harry. Before long, he would be celebrating his first anniversary as the Woo Dip's authentic Chinese chef. He loved his new job and was very fond of the family he had come to know. He enjoyed trying out his Chinese dishes on Lawney and Luana. He appreciated the expressions on their faces as they experienced the unusual food he served them.

When winter came and the snow fell, he loved taking the children out for walks on the wooden boardwalks. He helped them make their first snowman in the sandlot behind the restaurant. Harry had just as much fun as the children and Pickles when they played together in the snow. He had never been so happy.

In early spring 1937, shortly after the restaurant had closed for the day, Harry received some surprising news. Julian and Mary had decided to move back to Inchelium at the end of May. Lawney would be starting school in the fall, and Mary wanted him to go to school in Inchelium. The little town that had been their home for so many years would soon be covered with water when the dam was completed. Mary and Julian wanted to live there for as long as they could before that happened. They would then have to move their home to higher ground up in the hills.

And there was another reason. Mary was expecting a baby in September, and she wanted the infant to be born in Inchelium.

Harry was surprised by what Mary was telling him. He was happy about the new child but not so happy that the family would be leaving B Street. He was not pleased about what was going to happen to their little town. He had thought that the dam construction was good because it provided jobs for everyone who needed help. It had never occurred to him that harmful things could happen after it was built. Harry was sorry that Mary's people would suffer greatly because of the dam. But he was also concerned about the restaurant.

Julian and Mary knew that Harry was responsible for the restaurant's success. Harry had been important to them. Because of his efforts, they had saved enough money to last them for some time. Julian hoped Harry would accept their offer to sell the restaurant to him.

Harry pondered all this news with mixed feelings. He was disappointed that his friends would be leaving. Harry realized that they were the only friends he had. He would miss the children and their dog Pickles very much. But he was pleased by the realization that he would have his own business. This had always been his dream. Losing his best friends was the price he would have to pay for having that business.

At the end of May, the family climbed into the Model T. Harry had prepared a feast for them. It was the best meal they had ever had. He also packed several wrapped sandwiches to be eaten later. It proved to be a touching good-bye for everyone. The children had grown very close to Harry during their time together. They regarded him as a third parent. Harry had taught and shared his knowledge with them. They could not have received from anyone else the wisdom they received from their unassuming Chinese chef.

Harry knew it would be difficult to run the business without their help. He stood in front of the restaurant on B Street, watching his friends drive away. The children had tears in their eyes as they knelt in the back of the Model T, waving at Harry through the rear window. He could see Pickles barking his good-bye, standing on his hind legs with his front paws against the window. The Model T made a right turn and proceeded slowly down the hill to Midway Avenue. A rush of loneliness filled Harry.

A few customers followed Harry as he reentered the restaurant. He nodded to the new waitress as he went to the kitchen. He was glad that Mary had trained her before she left. He would have to depend on her heavily in the days that followed. Harry went about his business of cooking and planning the operation of the restaurant.

When the restaurant closed at 2:00 A.M., Harry sat alone in the dining room, smoking a cigarette. He drank his tea slowly, thinking about Julian and his family. He thought of Pickles. He would miss Lawney's and Luana's little friend. Harry smiled as he remembered how Pickles would howl when he hit high notes on his vio-

lin. It would be days before he could cope adequately with the loneliness he felt.

After Julian and the family left, Harry moved into the tent behind
the restaurant. It felt good to be in his friends' old home. He made
adjustments to suit his needs, and the place became his home.

One morning after closing, Harry picked up the menu Mary had
prepared. He studied the menu and smiled as he read the words
"Woo Dip." He wondered what Mary had been thinking when she
came up with that name. He smiled again, imagining the reactions
of other Chinese to the words "Woo Dip" on the sign outside the
restaurant. He thought about writing to friends in Canton to see if
they knew what the words meant but felt self-conscious about doing
so. The words appeared somewhat silly to him, yet he had to know
if they actually meant something in Chinese. Perhaps his acquain-
tances in China could help. In time, Harry would learn that the
words meant "butterfly" in certain Chinese dialects.

Harry decided to change the name. He found himself struggling
to come up with a unique Chinese name. Finally, he stood up and
stretched. He put out his cigarette in an ashtray on the table and
stood there thinking a while more, then shrugged. As he walked to
the tent, he decided that he would simply call his restaurant "Harry
Wong's Noodle Parlour."

Harry decided that he needed a new menu to go along with the
restaurant's new name. He thought it was time to add other, more
authentic Chinese dishes, such as sweet-and-sour spareribs and bok
choy and beef. Harry wanted to introduce these genuinely Chinese
dishes to his customers. He decided to add mandarin fried chicken
to the menu, also. It took more time to prepare but was very tasty.
Harry felt that his customers would learn to enjoy these foods. He
decided to order new sauces and spices from Chinatown, in Seat-

tle, along with bok choy and Chinese broccoli. As he thought about all of this, it suddenly occurred to him that for the first time in his entire life, he did not have to ask anyone's permission to make these changes. It felt good. He had to remind himself that he was the owner of Harry Wong's Noodle Parlour and was the one who would be making all the decisions.

As the days went on, Harry's spirits were lifted when people from Inchelium came to the restaurant. He was pleased when Edo and a friend came one night. They had met about a year ago, and he prepared an extra-special meal for them. Edo could see the loneliness in Harry's eyes, and it touched her. She suggested he take some time off and visit Julian and his family. Edo knew that Harry had never been on the reservation.

Harry lit a cigarette and thought a while. He went into the kitchen and put more wood in the cookstove. When he returned, he told Edo that he would go one day soon.

The Indians who came from Inchelium were usually broke. Life on the reservation had not improved, and it was as difficult as ever to survive. All had come to Grand Coulee in hopes of finding a job, any job.

Sometimes, they came to the restaurant in groups. Some would not order any food because they could not pay for it. When Harry sensed this, he would bring more food to the table and set out extra plates and chopsticks. Harry never charged his friends for the additional food he provided. He remembered what it was like to be poor. He had been poor most of his life. He was determined to help anyone who needed it and prevent them from suffering as he once had.

When he saw that his Indian friends had trouble with the chopsticks, he went into the kitchen and returned with silverware. He smiled as he observed that Indians were no better than white people when it came to eating with the prized utensils of his people.

Harry always measured his time in the same way. After closing, he made sure that everything was in order for the next day. He attended to any food that had to be prepared for the following day. Business was good. He had to hire another waitress to handle the increase in customers.

Harry realized he had to do something to occupy his free time. He reflected on his experiences in America. These were all new for him. Life was certainly much different in his new home, so far from China. He reasoned that if he told friends in China how he lived now, they would have a hard time believing him. The more Harry thought of this, the more intriguing it became for him.

The following day, as Harry worked, he could not forget his thoughts of the night before. He was a unique person in a foreign land. He was an important part of it all. Many people on B Street had grown to accept him. His friends in China would be amazed that he had survived. They would be surprised that he now owned a restaurant named after himself, Harry Wong's Noodle Parlour. He wished he could let them know of the life he was leading. He decided he would write short stories about his life in America. Harry knew there would be many stories about B Street alone.

So early in the morning, after work, Harry got a pot of tea and poured a cup. He lit a cigarette and thought for a while, sitting back in his chair and watching the smoke curl and make its way to the ceiling. His mind drifted, and then he bent over at the table and carefully wrote, in Chinese characters, short stories about his experiences in America. After weeks of concentration, he had a number of short stories, and he was satisfied with them. He mailed them to the publisher of a newspaper he knew in Canton.

Harry Wong at the Woo Dip restaurant, 1937. Courtesy Teresa Wong.

Weeks later, he received word that some of his stories were going to be published in the Canton newspaper. Harry was pleased with his efforts and continued to write other stories. This helped occupy his time when he felt alone. Sometimes, he experimented with poetry. He realized that he had a talent he had never known he had. A number of his poems were also published in Canton. Writing proved to be a good way to escape his loneliness when he was not working.

Aside from missing his dear friends, Harry was pleased with his lot in life. The restaurant continued to make money, and the people on B Street were friendly to him. The newspaper in Canton continued to print some of his written work. Most of all, he was glad that he could help his Indian friends from the little town of Inchelium, friends who were hungry. He would never forget the warm feelings that came to him when he offered food and goodwill to those people from the reservation who had faced years of deprivation caused by a government that was insensitive to their needs.

10

CEREMONY OF TEARS

Most of the work on the dam was completed toward the end of May 1940, and Harry learned that a number of Indian tribes who once fished at Kettle Falls planned to have a farewell gathering at the site. They wanted to do this before the river rose, and that time was drawing near. The farewell, the Ceremony of Tears, was to be a three-day event, beginning on June 14, to commemorate the loss of the most important asset the Indian tribes in the area had. The beautiful Kettle Falls was the center of culture for at least two tribes, the Sin-Aikst and the Swhy al puh, who had been its caretakers for centuries. But tribes from all over the Northwest and as far east as the Great Plains would be present. This would be the saddest day in the lives of the Indians who gathered there to pay tribute.

The event had been planned for months. Thousands of people, both Indian and white, were expected to attend to bid farewell to the Falls. Harry decided the time had come for him to visit the little town of Inchelium and see Kettle Falls before both were covered with water. He wanted to be a part of that last gathering. He could see that it would be a special event. The ceremony would mark the beginning of the end for the tribes who had always depended on the Falls for both physical and spiritual sustenance.

Friends from Inchelium volunteered to drive him north from B Street. Harry was delighted with the idea. He had never been to an Indian reservation and had always wanted to see the Falls. The trip would allow him to visit the children—Lawney, Luana, and their little brother, Bernard. He planned to bring them Chinese fruits and sweets that he had received from Canton. He remembered that Lawney and Luana had always liked the treats when they lived on B Street.

Harry studied his wardrobe and decided he needed clothes that would be more suitable for wear on the reservation. He made a list of what he needed and included a pair of walking boots and a hat to shade his eyes from the sun. A few days later, he went down to Grand Coulee and shopped. After finding everything he wanted, he walked up the hill to B Street and stopped in at Rawe's Hardware, where he bought a small canteen. It would come in handy to have drinking water if the weather got hot.

He was looking forward to the coming trip. This would be Harry's first vacation in more than three years. He was curious about Inchelium and Kettle Falls and wanted to see where his Indian friends lived. He wondered if any still lived in tepees, like Indians he had seen in movies. Mary had told him that many of her people rode horses. He had never seen a live horse up close and hoped he would see at least one.

Harry was all smiles as he got into the car. Moops Quill and his younger brother, Mike, were driving him to Inchelium. They rose early and left in the morning. The trip would take nearly three hours. Before arriving at Kettle Falls, Moops wanted Harry to visit Gold

Mountain, Twin Lakes, and Inchelium. As they prepared to leave, Dewey Hall came running up the street and asked Moops if there was room for him. Harry slid over in the backseat.

After passing through a small range of mountains east of Nespelem, they came to Cashe Creek and the San Poil River. Dewey advised Harry that this was rattlesnake country, and Harry did not seem impressed. Dewey asked Harry what he would do if he saw a rattlesnake. Harry answered, "Chop off head. Make chow mein. Snake good eat." Dewey removed the handmade smoke from his lips and turned his head away with a grimace.

When they reached Gold Mountain Summit, Moops pulled the car to one side, and they walked to the edge of the road to admire the scenery below. There were millions of trees and endless mountains. Harry was overwhelmed by the grandeur of it all.

Everyone returned to the car, and Moops carefully descended the mountain. The road was graveled, and he was aware that the car could jackknife and slide off the road. There were no guardrails to prevent them from going over the steep cliffs along the way. They reached Twin Lakes, and Harry was impressed by the beauty of North Twin. When they arrived at Rocky Point, Moops parked once again. Harry got out and studied the northern lake. He was awed by its size and beauty. He followed a trail and walked down to the lake. He bent down to touch the cool water and smiled.

Harry looked forward to seeing the children when they arrived at Julian's house near Cobb's Creek. Lawney and Luana were playing outside with Bernard. When the two older children recognized Harry, they ran to him and embraced him warmly. Harry had not seen Bernard before. He noticed how friendly he was. Harry was impressed with Bernard's demeanor and his dark piercing eyes that didn't seem to miss a thing. Harry studied Lawney and Luana and realized they had grown. Three years had passed quickly. He was pleased that they had a little brother to help keep them company. He marveled at how close they were. Harry gave them their box of Chinese candy and fruits and told them he was on his way to see Inchelium and Kettle Falls.

He looked at their little house surrounded by many trees and studied the adjoining property. The area looked as if no one had ever lived there. The narrow trails carved through the field of wild grass by the children were the only sign of people. Harry was impressed with the little creek flowing by. The area was clean, quiet, and peaceful, so unlike B Street. He smiled and thought that Julian and Mary had chosen a good setting for their little home.

He learned that Julian was now working on a Works Progress Administration crew. The men's job was to cut down all the trees that would be covered by water after the area was flooded. Then the logs were floated downriver to the small town of Hunters, where they were cut into lumber.

After visiting with the children for half an hour, it was time to leave. Harry knew the day would be filled with many activities at the Falls, and he didn't want to miss any of them. He asked the children to give his regards to their father. Lawney and Luana embraced Harry again as they said their good-byes. Bernard walked up to Harry, smiling, and offered his hand.

Moops started the car and drove slowly down a winding dirt road. The river came into view. Harry could see that it was already rising. Huge banks of earth had fallen into the water. Old logs, pieces of weather-beaten boards, and other debris were floating very slowly down the river, and the water was beginning to look muddy along the shore. Harry imagined what this once powerful and pristine river must have looked like only days before, and the change saddened him.

Moops alerted Harry as they entered Main Street, in Inchelium.

Harry saw that it was nearly deserted. Only a few homes remained. Most of the sturdier houses had already been moved. Harry could see the large building with the raised boardwalk in front that had been the General Store. It, too, was deserted. He remembered Mary and Julian talking often about this building. The area resembled a ghost town. It wouldn't be long before the river rose to cover everything.

Harry noticed the water pump standing in the middle of Main Street. He walked over and pumped some water, caught some in his hands, and drank. The water tasted cold and fresh. Moops, Mike, Dewey, and Harry walked along the street, looking in the windows of old, vacant houses. They studied the weathered wood-block foundations where houses had once stood. Harry looked at the tree-covered benches above town and saw in the distance a man riding a horse slowly along a hillside. The scene reminded him of a western movie about Indians he had once seen.

Dewey pointed to an empty lot. That was where Julian and his family had once lived. They had moved their house in February when there was still snow on the ground. Some men had put the house on log skids and pulled it with a small Caterpillar to the property by the little creek where they had just visited the children.

After Julian and his family were settled, he came back to help others in town move the graves in the cemetery to higher ground, up in the hills. It took about two months. Hall Creek Cemetery was the new burial ground.

As Harry studied the surroundings, he understood the poverty his Indian friends were going through. Everything looked old. It was like stepping back into another century. He had faced much poverty in his life, but these people were facing even more. Their misfortune saddened him.

As they walked farther south, past the ball field, they saw a

One of the general stores in Inchelium, before the flooding (top).
Courtesy of Kathy DeSautel and Trudi Tonasket.

Inchelium school building during the flooding of the town.
Courtesy of Carl Putnam and Trudi Tonasket.

schoolhouse a short distance away. The large building appeared to be floating in the river.

"Why in water?" Harry asked.

Moops explained, "We just ran out of time. The Bureau of Reclamation agreed to lower the river so we could move the school to higher ground. We had to anchor it with dozens of sandbags so it wouldn't float away. You can see some of them in the entry."

Now and then, rumbling sounds could be heard, like distant thunder. Harry learned that these sounds were caused by banks and cliffs falling into the river as it rose. The noise sounded ominous to him.

Moops continued to drive north along the Columbia River to Kettle Falls. Dewey put his cigarette out in the ashtray and explained that there used to be many salmon in the river, but they were gone now. When the greater part of the dam was built in 1938, it stopped all salmon from going upriver. Before that, less than three hundred reached Kettle Falls because of the dam at Rock Island. Now there were only whitefish, perch, and a few other species that no one cared to eat. Most of the sturgeon were down deep near Kettle Falls. They got very large, some more than twelve feet in length.

After traveling another thirty miles, they arrived at Kettle Falls. Harry was impressed by the large number of people and their solemn and purposeful demeanor. Most of the eight thousand who had gathered were Indians of various tribes. Everyone was quiet and respectful. A number stood along the banks of the river and studied the magnificent falls thundering over the huge rocks. The Falls were all that Harry had expected. He had not witnessed such beauty and power anywhere else before.

There were many tepees and tents on both sides of the river, and a great number of horses grazed close to the encampments. Harry

Kettle Falls circa 1938. Courtesy The Spokesman-Review.

had never seen anything like this, not even in movies. Here and there, white people were taking photographs as Indians posed. None of the Indians smiled.

Harry knew that the Indians had come to celebrate the Ceremony of Tears, a tribute to the beautiful Falls that had been the center of the Sin-Aikst and Swhy al puh cultures for centuries. It saddened him to think all this would be gone within days.

He walked with Dewey to a forested area. A large white-painted altar of wood had been placed among the Ponderosa pines to serve as a place of worship for those who were Catholic. Harry could appreciate the beautiful setting. Hundreds of Indians were gathered there for a midday Mass. Many were praying out loud in their own language, holding rosary beads. Harry saw Mary standing among them. She appeared a little older now. She was standing with her best friend, Edo. Harry and his three friends stood among the pines, respectfully waiting for the ceremony to end.

Mary and Edo were pleased to see that Harry had made the trip. They walked over to greet him. Mary suggested that they get a closer look at the Falls, and they walked to the banks of the river. Harry recognized a number of Indians who had come to his restaurant. They greeted one another warmly. As they talked, Mary and Harry had to shout in order to be heard because of the noise that came from the Falls. They walked away from the river so that they could talk without shouting, and Mary explained the history of the Falls.

"During the month of June each year," she told Harry, "the great assembly of Indian tribes arrived. It was then that the chinook made their way upriver to spawn. They came in great numbers. The strongest of the chinook could jump the Falls and continue upriver in search of tributaries where they could spawn. Those salmon unable to clear the Falls were caught in nets and traps. Others were speared.

"When the chinook came in June, the Salmon Chief stood in the water below the Falls and blessed them. He welcomed them and thanked them for coming to feed the People. He would not allow salmon to be caught until he was satisfied that enough had cleared the Falls to spawn upriver. That would ensure the survival of the species. When the time came, he would be the first to spear a salmon, signaling the beginning of the season. The Salmon Chief's responsibility was to make sure each tribe got a fair share at the end of each day. Many tribes came: the Spokane, the Coeur d'Alene, the

Nespelem, the Okanogan, the Swhy al puh, the Wenatchee, the Sin-Aikst, the San Poil, the Entiat, the Methow, and others.

"Nets and traps were used to catch the salmon. Only the most daring of the fishermen would stand above the falls on extended planks and spear the salmon as they prepared to jump. That type of fishing was very dangerous. The fisherman had to be very strong and agile. Many of the chinook weighed more than one hundred pounds and were very powerful. The largest ever caught was 125 pounds. If someone lost his balance and fell in, he would usually be overwhelmed by the rapids and drown. The water was swift, and the currents were very strong, powerful enough to pull a person under.

"In earlier years, during the mid-nineteenth century, a number of Plains Indians came to trade dried buffalo meat and hides for the salmon. Some were Blackfeet, others were Flathead from western Montana. They arrived astride beautiful horses, attracting the interest of the Plateau Indians, who were native to the region. The Plains Indians were skilled craftsmen, and their attire, beautifully adorned with beads and quillwork, attracted much attention. Visitors also admired and traded for other items of interest, like spears, bows and arrows, tomahawks, and knives.

"When the tribes came to harvest the chinook, they camped on both sides of the river. Tepees of the different tribes were everywhere. Horses accompanied them and grazed close to the tepees and the grasslands beyond. Wagons were parked near the tepees.

"During the day, the beautiful sturgeon-nosed canoes of the Upper Sin-Aikst traveled back and forth in great numbers, crossing the river. The canoes were distinctive in their design, with their noses slanting down. Because of their low center of gravity, they sat deep in the water. They were a beautiful sight to behold."

Tears came briefly to Mary's eyes as she realized she would never witness this again. With a heavy sigh, she pointed northeast to the main island of the lower Falls. "That's where my people used to camp and wind-dry the salmon. That was the best way to preserve them. The taste was always best when they were prepared in that manner."

Harry saw Antoine Paul and Eneas Boyd standing in a clearing next to their horses. He remembered Eneas working at the dam and recalled that he was a very capable prizefighter. Antoine had brought the horses from Inchelium to Kettle Falls in the back of his truck. Harry was delighted. He had never seen a real horse before, only in photographs and movies. They fascinated him. Realizing this, Mary led him up to Antoine's bay. She encouraged Harry to pet the horse and not be afraid. The horse would like the attention.

Harry cautiously touched the bay's forehead, then proceeded to pet him. A big grin appeared on his face. He was pleased to be able to touch the bay. He thought horses were the most beautiful animals on earth. It felt good to be close to one.

After bidding Mary good-bye, Antoine and Eneas mounted their horses and rode up into the mountains. Harry was impressed with how easily they rode. It looked as if they were a part of their horses, in perfect balance with every move.

Harry learned that they were going to visit some of their ancestors who were buried up in the hills. There was always a feeling

(Opposite, top) *At one time, Sin-Aikst sturgeon-nosed canoes came in great numbers from upriver to Kettle Falls. Courtesy Arrow Lakes Historical Society, Nakusp, British Columbia.*

(Opposite, bottom) *Sin-Aikst Indian spearfishing for chinook at Kettle Falls, 1938. Courtesy Northwest Museum of Arts & Culture, Spokane.*

among the People that descendants were an extension of those who passed away. As long as there were descendants, a part of life would continue without end. Harry nodded in understanding.

Harry stood next to Mary, deep in thought. He had never imagined that there were so many different Indians. He used to think there was only one tribe. As he studied the Falls, he found it hard to believe that it would one day be gone. He had the idea that when the salmon were gone, the Indians might also disappear. These thoughts bothered Harry. Over the years, he had learned to like Mary's people. He was glad to have such friends.

As Harry followed Mary around the site, he met more Indians who had come to B Street. They were happy to see Harry and remembered his generosity. They recalled that he would bring out extra food from the kitchen so that everyone would have something to eat. The Indians remembered how good the food was. When they could afford it, they would always return to B Street to experience his fine cooking.

Throughout the day, Harry observed other ritualistic ceremonies performed by groups of Indians representing different tribes. Through it all, the gathering maintained its solemn demeanor. As the sun was setting, he and Mary walked the area near the Falls once again and looked out over the beautiful scenery. It was time for Harry to return to his restaurant on B Street.

Before Harry left, Mary insisted that he experience traditional Sin-Aikst staples: bitterroot, camas, and dried huckleberries. She wanted him to enjoy the smoked salmon prepared by the elders using bent willow branches to form a canopy over a hot fire. Harry found the food unique, much different from his accustomed foods. He especially enjoyed the salmon. The seasoned smoke created a flavor that was new to him.

Suddenly, loud voices accompanied by singing and drumming

Sin-Aikst and Colville Indians at the Ceremony of Tears, 1940.
Courtesy Northwest Museum of Arts & Culture, Spokane.

Sin-Aikst women smoking salmon on bentwood branches during
the Ceremony of Tears, 1940. Courtesy Northwest Museum of Arts
& Culture, Spokane.

caught Harry's attention. A large group of Indians was playing a game he had never seen before. Edo told him Indians had played this game at traditional events for centuries. It was a form of gambling, accompanied by singing and the striking of sticks on a long pole placed in front of the players, called the Stick Game. Others stood behind the players, singing and drumming in perfect cadence on small hand drums. It was a game of deception in which intuition played an important role.

Harry observed the two teams seated in two rows facing each other. Edo explained that each team had two sets of bones, one unmarked and the other taped. The object of the game seemed to be to guess which hand of a person on the opposing team concealed the unmarked bones. Edo claimed the rules of the game were few, but Harry had a hard time keeping up with the fast action of hand

Sin-Aikst and Colville Indians playing the Stick Game at the Ceremony of Tears, 1940. Courtesy University of Washington Libraries.

signals and yelps from the participants, especially when they began to use the sticks. The excitement of the game drew him in. Harry wished he could stay longer. He had always enjoyed gambling. As he observed, the players seemed to be in a sort of a trance. It was as if they were in another world, a spiritual world. This interested him very much. But Moops was signaling him that it was time to return to B Street.

They seated themselves in the car, and Harry was delighted when his driver presented him with a small paper sack filled with dried huckleberries, bitterroot, and camas.

For days after returning to B Street, Harry recalled his trip to the reservation and the beauty and power of Kettle Falls. He was grateful he had been able to see those places before they were gone. Harry was pleased that he had visited his dear friends, the children, and happy that they were healthy and had grown. He appreciated the sincerity and warmth with which his Indian friends had welcomed him. They were all good people. How lucky he was to have such fine friends! He would remember his trip to the reservation and the things he had seen there for the rest of his life.

Early one morning, Harry sat in the dining room studying the sack of dried huckleberries, bitterroot, and camas. He had tried pieces of the roots, and they reminded him of the ones his people had gathered for medicinal purposes in China.

Harry's thoughts went back to Kettle Falls. How beautiful the area was to him. He had never seen anything so wonderful. He could easily live in such a place forever. The Indian people were lucky to have had such a place and unlucky now that they were to lose it. He had experienced misfortunes in his life more than once. But they had only affected him personally, and he had learned to cope with them. His Indian friends were soon to experience something more devastating, an experience that, through no fault of their own, would hurt them all. It would be a total loss of something dear to all of them, their sense of well-being, their culture, and, finally, their identity. He wondered why white people found it necessary to shatter and usurp the cultures of others in order to reap personal gain.

The construction of Grand Coulee Dam had been a godsend for Harry. It had enabled him to find work at a Chinese restaurant and, finally, to own it. He was now an entrepreneur. This had been his most important goal in life. His time on B Street had made it possible for him to make and save money. He had more money now than ever before.

But he grieved when he thought about what Grand Coulee Dam had done to Julian, Mary, and the children. He worried about his other Indian friends. The construction of this mighty edifice had destroyed everything of value for them. It would take away their homes, their land, and their most valuable source of food, Kettle Falls. These thoughts lingered with Harry and distressed him.

Harry vowed that he would do as much as he could to help Indians in need while he was in business on B Street. He knew that the construction of the dam was nearing completion and that one day soon he would have to move and set up a business elsewhere. But he was confident. He had learned the business of running a restaurant well during the last four years.

During the late summer of 1940, the number of workingmen on B Street dwindled. People in business could tell that construction was nearing completion, and work on the dam would soon be phased out. They wondered how much longer their businesses could survive. Many dreaded the day when the dam would be completed.

Harry saw that businesses on both sides of the street were beginning to close. He knew that his own business was slowing down.

Many of the pretty ladies were no longer coming to the restaurant. Many had returned to their hometowns, and others were living in the larger cities of Seattle, Spokane, and Tacoma. It made him sad to observe the empty buildings that used to bustle with excitement. The boardwalk, once filled with people, was becoming deserted. The loud music that had come from the many taverns and dance halls was gone. Everyone would miss the good times on The Street.

He was pleased that Mom Pozar's place was still open, although her restaurant was beginning to show the effects of the end of construction. He had heard that it was one of the first businesses to open on The Street. He remembered seeing her when times were better as he took his walks. She always waved to him with a friendly smile.

Harry knew that he would soon have to close his restaurant and move to a new location, perhaps west of the mountains. There was not enough business for him to stay. He was disappointed at the thought that he would have to leave B Street. He had grown to like the area and the people who lived there. Harry had adjusted to the climate and appreciated the change of seasons. He did not look forward to all the rain on the Washington coast.

On August 27, 1940, unknown to Harry, Lawney and Luana passed through Grand Coulee. They were on their way to the Chemawa Indian Boarding School in Oregon, as decreed by court order. Earlier that day, Julian had brought the children to Nespelem, where they were loaded into the back of an open truck with fifteen other Indian children. They would be driven more than four hundred miles to Chemawa that afternoon.

It was about 4:30 P.M. when the truck passed through Grand Coulee. In a few hours, the sun would set. Harry did not know that the children were thinking about him as they passed through the town. He did not know that the children were afraid, uncertain, and unaware of where they were going or how long they would be gone. Harry did not know that they would soon be cold and hungry, riding in an uncovered truck to a place far away in Oregon. He did not know the children would never visit him again on B Street. Years would pass before he would see them again, when they were grown, at another place in another time.

EPILOGUE

Toward the end of 1940, the dam was nearing completion. Daily progress was clear from just viewing the dam. Everyone was awed by the size of the huge concrete structure. When the construction reached this stage, the men knew that work forces would be reduced. Within a short time, only a small number remained on the payroll to put the finishing touches on the dam. Some of the workers returned to their hometowns in Washington State and across the country. Others went elsewhere to seek work. Eventually, many of these adventurous, fun-loving young men would be needed again when the Japanese bombed Pearl Harbor, in the Hawaiian Islands, on December 7, 1941. During late 1941, many of these happy-go-lucky stiffs would go forth and fight against great odds in the Pacific and across the Atlantic. They were part of what became known as the Greatest Generation.

With the departure of the workers, most of the pretty ladies moved on as well. Some would marry, have kids, and lead a conventional life. Many others would find work on the Northwest Coast. These women would one day perform the work of men in huge factories and shipyards in western Washington and Oregon, helping immeasurably during World War II.

When the workmen and the pretty ladies left B Street, businesses along the boardwalks closed. A few tried to make a go of it, but in time they, too, had to shut their doors. Everyone knew that the great days of The Street were over. The empty buildings that lined both sides of the thoroughfare were all that was left of one of the wildest streets in America. Only memories would remain, and within years they would gradually fade away.

A large crowd of white people assembled to celebrate the completion of the dam in 1941. Nearly a dozen Indians in warbonnets were also there, with perplexed expressions on their usually stoic faces. Politicians and local leaders made many speeches that day. They praised themselves for the part they had played in placing the huge concrete monolith across the once mighty river.

Jim James of the Colvilles, whom some considered a chief, was selected to turn the switch that would start the great turbines and complete the damming of the river. He smiled timidly, appearing pleased that his photograph would appear in the newspapers. His presence at this event suggested that he had little understanding of and concern for his people, who were losing their homes, their land, their resources, the great river—the Swah net ka—and their beloved culture and way of life.

After the dam was completed, for a short time a few businesses on B Street stubbornly resisted closing. A tavern stayed open, as did a small restaurant. Rawe's Hardware served the needs of the few who lived in and near the area. A small cadre of working stiffs appeared at night after their workday at the dam, looking for excitement and recreation. And a few pretty ladies remained to serve the dwindling number of workers and the occasional tourists passing through.

Grand Coulee Dam's completion celebration, with Colville Indian delegation and spectators, 1941. Courtesy Northwest Museum of Arts & Culture, Spokane.

Later, Negroes came to The Street, which had always been off-limits to them. They set up a few houses of prostitution that employed a small number of Negro women. Again, they experienced prejudice and realized that times had not really changed. There was not enough business to make it worth their while, and they finally packed up and left.

Life on B Street continued into the mid-fifties. Mom Pozar kept her restaurant open for business until she died at a very old age. Mom's was the last business remaining on The Street, and its closing marked the end of an era.

Years later, visitors to B Street would leave Midway Avenue and go up the hill to the bench. Along the way, they would see more than a hundred hardhats of various colors fastened to a wooden fence near A Street, left behind by men who had completed their work at the dam. The hats were a silent salute to more than seven thousand working men who were employed at the dam site during its heyday. It was also a reminder that seventy-seven workers had lost their lives during construction.

Midway Avenue is now bordered by an odd assortment of buildings and is continuously traveled by residents of Grand Coulee and the small communities surrounding it. It is a thoroughfare for tourists coming to see the great dam, after traveling on what was once known as the Speedball Highway. The pace of life is much slower now; everything is quiet. Few would remember that from 1933 through 1940, B Street was probably the noisiest street in America.

It is difficult to imagine what B Street looked like in the 1930s, with hundreds, sometimes thousands, assembled there. The noise from the many loudspeakers in competing taverns and dancehalls was once so loud that people had to shout to be heard. Today, the sounds of working stiffs clomping in heavy work boots and the staccato tap of the high heels of the pretty ladies are no longer heard. The quiet goes unchallenged. The only light comes from fixtures high up on a few poles that cast a surreal and haunting glow. The occasional sounds and some movement come only when gentle winds sweep the quiet street.

Over the years, the people who fostered the idea of the dam have been acclaimed and applauded. Those who designed and constructed the massive edifice also received due credit, but today they are nearly forgotten. The thousands of workers who built the dam and faced constant danger during construction have become nameless. The pretty ladies who left their indelible imprint on B Street are gone and remembered by only a few. The legacy of these adventurous people becomes fainter as each year passes.

As a result of the Grand Coulee Dam, a half million acres of dry land, once covered by sagebrush and tumbleweeds, are now irrigated and produce a variety of crops that feed millions. The power generated by the dam undoubtedly contributed greatly to victory in World War II. The energy was indispensable to manufacturers of aircraft, ships, and other arms and equipment designed for war. The great quantities of planes and ships could not have been manufactured so quickly without it. The Boeing Airplane Company and shipyards in the Seattle-Bremerton area and Portland, Oregon, depended heavily on power supplied by the dam. And the Hanford Engineer Works, which supplied plutonium for the atomic bombs that were dropped on Japan in 1945, relied on power from Grand Coulee Dam.

The construction of the dam provided various forms of employment to at least ten thousand people who engaged in their different trades on and around B Street. Many had suffered greatly during the Depression and might have starved or ended their lives in desperation if not for their jobs at the dam.

But there is another side to this story—the loss of what was once the greatest salmon run in the world. It is important to realize that construction of the Grand Coulee Dam cut off approximately eleven hundred miles of salmon spawning grounds in the Columbia River. The salmon coming upriver by the millions tried to penetrate the steel and concrete barrier that lay between them and their traditional spawning areas, which stretched across 150 miles and were fed by numerous tributaries. All the salmon perished. This proved to be the signal that the great days were ending and that the lifestyle for all who were a part of the river would change.

For centuries, Indian tribes had depended on the river for sustenance and spiritual powers. With the dam, much of the land that produced the best edible roots and berries was submerged under water, along with important and beautiful landmarks. Much of this great land and everything that grew on it were lost to the People forever. Finally, Kettle Falls was buried, and the great river itself was gone. The beautiful sights the river created are lost to future generations who will never witness or fully understand the power, splendor, and beauty that once was.

Authorities from the Bureau of Reclamation have been questioned as to why they did not build fish ladders for the salmon but give no satisfying answers. Some say it would have been too expensive. Others say it would have been impossible because of the force of the river and the height of the dam. The young salmon, they say, would have been killed as they migrated downriver. However, another authority states that if a dam of this size could have been built, then a fish ladder surely could have been built as well.

In truth, officials at the Bureau of Reclamation did take steps to preserve the salmon, but they initially believed that the dam's economic contributions far outweighed the value of preserving fish. For more than three years, the bureau squabbled with the U.S. Department of Fisheries and Washington State officials over salmon preservation but reached no conclusions. Salmon were caught, put in tanks at the Rock Island Dam, and transported to Leavenworth, Washington, where hatcheries were constructed. The Department of Fisheries attempted to hatch salmon, but there was never enough water to fill the pools, and many young salmon died. Some of the salmon that survived were transported to tributaries in the hope that they might adjust to new spawning places, while others were placed above Grand Coulee Dam with the same idea in mind. Many times, these efforts failed, and the salmon would never again match the great runs that existed before the dam was built.

At this time, the Canadian government was not concerned about salmon because Canada had no commercial fisheries on the Columbia River in British Columbia. Government officials did not envision the wealth that salmon could bring to the country and felt that the dam would have no adverse effect on the fish. The provincial government of British Columbia was not involved with efforts to preserve the salmon.

It seems safe to assume that the only reason the salmon were not saved is that no one in authority at the time thought they were important. Only a few white people in eastern Washington valued salmon as a food. Many believed that only Indians ate these fish and had no idea of how important salmon would become to everyone as a nutritional staple.

Authorities from the Bureau of Reclamation and other U.S. government officials turned a deaf ear to questions about the welfare of Columbia River Indians. They hastened to change the subject; it was as if they had never heard of Indians. These members of the dominant culture were interested only in their own goals and their own way of life. Unique and important cultures that had lived in harmony with nature for thousands of years were dismissed as victims of progress.

Before the dam was constructed, the federal government promised the Colville Indians free electricity. After the dam was completed, members of the tribe ended up paying the highest rates in the state. The government promised the Colvilles canned salmon in payment for the salmon lost at Kettle Falls, but the supplies were seldom delivered.

In 1977, Lucy Covington, a respected member of the Colville Confederated Tribal Council, stated: "We had a beautiful way of life. We were rich. The dam made us poor. The way they treated us, they tried to make us less than human. We Indians trust the day is past when the nation will approve of what the government did when it built the dam. The promises made by the government were written in sand and then washed away and covered with water when the river rose."

In 1941, the communities and towns of Inchelium, Gifford, Daisy, Kettle Falls, Marcus, Plum, Peach, Gerome, Lincoln, and Keller were flooded. What was lost there could never be replaced. The traditional burial grounds in Inchelium, Kettle Falls, Keller, and other places along the Columbia River were moved to higher ground. But many unmarked graves, located near the residences of Indian families along the river, were covered by water when the Columbia River rose. When this happened, a tradition centuries old was soon erased.

Elders who lived along the river and were physically unable to move their homes stayed until the water began to rise. The flooding forced them to leave their beloved homesteads and move to higher ground. They had only tents and teepees for shelter. In time, many died of grief over the loss of their homes and the gravesites of their ancestors.

According to Jim DeSautel, a Colville tribal member, "the River was the central and most powerful element in the religious, social, economic, and ceremonial life of my people. Suddenly, all of this was wiped out. The River was blocked and the land was flooded. The River we had known was destroyed. Our home sites were gone. Fording was made impossible. The far banks were beyond our reach. Root-digging prairies were cut off. The salmon came no more, and with the disappearance of the salmon, our traditional economy was lost forever."

After the completion of the Grand Coulee Dam, Al Auberton, chairman of the Colville Confederated Tribes, described the tribes' feelings about the dam: "The dam did not do anything good for us.

Aerial view of the present-day Grand Coulee Dam and surrounding communities. Courtesy Dennis King Photography.

Therese Kennedy Johns across the street from where the Silver Dollar Club once stood, 2007. Courtesy Lawney Reyes.

It destroyed our lifestyle and most of our resources. It took us sixty years to realize payment from the U.S. government for the connection of the east end of the dam to Colville Reservation property. All of the elders, and most who were adults then in our tribe, died before payment was made. We did not benefit from the building of the dam."

After the water rose to cover Inchelium, Kettle Falls, and other home sites, Nancy St. Paul Picard, a descendant of Cashmere St. Paul, stood along the west bank of the river. She studied the dirt road that led from her home, now underwater, up the hill to the west bench. She told friends, "I howled in grief when I saw a part of my family's home partially visible beneath the water. It had a ghostly appearance as I looked at it. The scene reminded me of death.

Our family spent so many unforgettable years in that great old house. That is where I was raised."

In traditional times, the Great Spirit provided everything that was needed to sustain life for all beings. Fresh sweet water was found in the lakes, rivers, and streams. The air was pure and clear. Pristine forests were everywhere. Food was usually plentiful and uncontaminated. And the land displayed a natural beauty that no artist could capture with chisel or paintbrush.

Over the centuries, tremendous forces triggered cataclysmic physical changes, and hard times, disease, famine, and violence sometimes followed. Life was never easy, and there were always great challenges. But over all this time, many humans have disregarded the wonders of this planet. Ignorance and greed have changed, destroyed, even poisoned things that were beautiful and necessary for a simple and wholesome existence.

After the arrival of the first white man more than a hundred years ago, things indeed changed on the once gentle but unnoticed bench. But in the twenty-first century, there are hints that other changes are taking place. The sagebrush, tumbleweeds, and cheatgrass at the edges of B Street seem ready to reclaim the landscape they once covered.

On a late afternoon, just before dark, a long-legged jackrabbit lopes along the hill covered with sagebrush. When it reaches the street, it stops and rests, with its long ears askew. It sits quietly on the empty lot where the Silver Dollar once entertained, with ear-splitting raucous music, a multitude of roughnecks and ladies of the night. At first glance, the ungainly animal, with its long legs and oversize feet, appears to be in a jocular mood. Closer observation reveals that it is thoughtfully studying the area. One can sense that it somehow belongs there, that it might have once lived there.

It seems predictable and logical that the jackrabbit, along with the coyotes, rattlesnakes, sage hens, ground squirrels, and other beings that make up a wonderful community of nature, are also ready to reclaim what was once theirs. The strangely proportioned jackrabbit seems to be smiling as it sits there. It is serving notice, to anyone who is interested, that as soon as the sagebrush and tumbleweeds grow back, the beings of yesteryear will return.

The sun sets and dusk steals over the water. In the shadows I seem again to see our Indian village, with smoke curling upward from the earth lodges, and in the river's roar I hear the yells of the warriors and the laughter of little children, as of old. It is but an old woman's dream. Then I see but shadows and hear only the roar of the river, and tears come into my eyes. Our Indian life, I know, is gone forever.

— WAHEENEE, HIDATSA (NORTH DAKOTA)

RESOURCES

PERSONAL INTERVIEWS

Chuck and Linda Hall, April 2002
Rod Hartman, September 2005
Dennis King, April 2002
Bill Miller, April 2002
Jean and Jack Nicholson, May 2001
Jean Nicholson, August 2002
Trudi Tonasket, August 2004

REFERENCES

Aguilar, George W., Sr. *When the River Ran Wild! Indian Traditions on the Mid-Columbia and the Warm Springs Reservation.* Portland: Oregon Historical Society Press; Seattle: University of Washington Press, 2005.

Bicentennial Association. *From Pioneers to Power: Historical Sketches of the Grand Coulee Dam Area.* Grand Coulee, Wash.: Grand Coulee Dam Bicentennial Association, 1976.

Blonk, Hu. *Behind the By-line.* Wenatchee, Wash.: Hu Blonk, 1992.

Harden, Blaine. *A River Lost: The Life and Death of the Columbia.* New York: W. W. Norton, 1996.

Meinig, D. W. *The Great Columbia Plain: An Historical Geography, 1805–1910*. Seattle: University of Washington Press, 1995.

Morgan, Murray. *The Dam*. New York: Viking Press, 1954.

Neuberger, Richard. *Our Promised Land*. Moscow: University of Idaho Press, 1989.

Pitzer, Paul. *Grand Coulee: Harnessing a Dream*. Pullman: Washington State University Press, 1994.

Reyes, Lawney L. *White Grizzly Bear's Legacy: Learning to Be Indian*. Seattle: University of Washington Press, 2002.

———. *Bernie Whitebear: An Urban Indian's Quest for Justice*. Tucson: University of Arizona Press, 2006.

Yakama Indian Nation. "Price We Paid." Videotape. Colville, Wash.: Media Services Colville, 1977.

NEWSPAPER ARTICLES

"Building Program on the Run." *Wenatchee Daily World*, October 16, 1933.

"Ferryman Throttles Action." *Wenatchee Daily World*, March 8, 1933.

"Governor Commission Vice Charges." *Wenatchee Daily World*, June 17, 1937.

"Grand Coulee Cleans House." *Wenatchee Daily World*, September 18, 1935.

"Hundreds Apply: Business Permits." *Wenatchee Daily World*, July 4, 1934.

"Mushroom City Springs to Life." *Wenatchee Daily World*, November 4, 1933.

"O'Sullivan on the Run." *Wenatchee Daily World*, January 19, 1933.

"Roosevelt at Grand Coulee." *Wenatchee Daily World*, August 4, 1934.

"Roosevelt Views Coulee Dam." *Wenatchee Daily World*,
    October 2, 1937.
"Vice Charges Exaggerated." *Wenatchee Daily World*,
    June 10, 1937.
World Commission on Dams (W.C.D.). "Coulee Dam Revisited."
    Oregonian, January 24, 2000.
———. "World Commission on Dams Study, Grand Coulee."
    Oregonian, February 16, 1999.

ONLINE RESOURCES

http://content.lib.washington.edu
http://www.dams.org
http://www.denniskingphoto.com
http://www.firstnations.com
http://www.historylink.org
http://www.Wikipedia.org

LIBRARY OF CONGRESS CATALOGING-IN-PUBLICATION DATA

Reyes, Lawney L.

B Street : the notorious playground of Coulee Dam /
    Lawney L. Reyes.

p. cm.

Includes bibliographical references.

ISBN 978-0-295-98853-5 (pbk. : alk. paper)

1. Colville Indians—History.

2. Colville Indians—Government relations.

3. Colville Indian Reservation (Wash.)—History.

4. Grand Coulee Dam (Wash.)—History.

5. Water resources development—Columbia River
    Watershed—History.

6. Grand Coulee (Wash.)—History.

7. Grand Coulee (Wash.)—Ethnic relations. I. Title.

E99.C844.R49 2008   979.7'31—dc22   2008006066

Photo by Therese Kennedy Johns

LAWNEY L. REYES graduated from the University of Washington in 1959 after attending the Chemawa Indian School in Oregon. A former art director for the Seafirst Corporation and a member of the Seattle Arts Commission, he has won numerous awards, including a Peace and Friendship Award for contributions to American Indian Art, a Washington Governor's Award for sculpture, and a Distinguished Alumnus Award from the University of Washington. He is the author of *White Grizzly Bear's Legacy: Learning to Be Indian* and *Bernie Whitebear: An Urban Indian's Quest for Justice.* He lives in Seattle.